TABLE OF CONTENTS

ACRONYMS

A2/AD	Anti-Access/Area Denial
ADCAP	Advanced Capability
AIP	Air Independent Propulsion
AOR	Area of Responsibility
APL	Applied Physics Laboratory
ASCM	Anti-Ship Cruise Missile
ASEAN	Association of Southeast Asian Nations
ASUW	Anti-Surface Warfare
ASW	Anti-Submarine Warfare
BUR	Bottom Up Review
C3	Command, Control, and Communications
CBASS	Common Broadband Advanced Sonar System
CBG	Carrier Battle Group
CBSA	Center for Strategic and Budgetary Assessments
CJCS	Chairman of the Joint Chiefs of Staff
CMSI	Chinese Maritime Studies Institute
COMPACFLT	Commander, Pacific Fleet
CS	Continental Shelf
CSG	Carrier Strike Group
CSIS	Center for Strategic and International Studies
CSS	Commander, Submarine Squadron
CZ	Contiguous Zone
DDG	Guided Missile Destroyer
DOD	Department of Defense
EEZ	Economic Exclusion Zone
ESG	Expeditionary Strike Group

FFG	Guided Missile Frigate
JCS	Joint Chiefs of Staff
JHU	Johns Hopkins University
KMT	Kuomintang
MPA	Maritime Patrol Aircraft
NATO	North Atlantic Treaty Organization
nm	nautical mile
NMS	National Military Strategy
NSS	National Security Strategy
NWC	Naval War College
ONI	Office of Naval Intelligence
OPREP	Operations Report
PLA	People's Liberation Army
PLAN	People's Liberation Army Navy
POTUS	President of the United States
PRC	People's Republic of China
QDR	Quadrennial Defense Review
ROE	Rules of Engagement
SCS	South China Sea
SECDEF	Secretary of Defense
SLBM	Submarine Launched Ballistic Missile
SLOC	Sea Lines of Communication
SSBN	Nuclear Ballistic Missile Submarine
SSGN	Nuclear Guided Missile Submarine
SSK	Diesel-Electric Submarine
SSN	Nuclear Fast Attack Submarine
SUBFOR	U.S. Submarine Force

TLAM	Tomahawk Land Attack Missile
UNCLOS	United Nations Convention on the Law of the Sea
USG	United States Government
USPACOM	United States Pacific Command
USSR	Union of Soviet Socialist Republics
WPTO	Western Pacific Theater of Operation

ILLUSTRATIONS

INTRODUCTION

> For the submarine community, you might say these are the best of times, and the worst of times – or if you prefer, that this is the year of living dangerously.
> — Ronald O'Rourke, Luncheon Address at JHU/APL

With the decline on the horizon of a more than a decade of costly U.S. involvement in persistent conflict throughout the Middle East, budgetary concerns inevitably led the United States Government (USG) to reexamine its national strategic policy. The 2011 National Security Strategy (NSS) stressed the importance of maintaining continued protection of the global commons in an effort to "prevent renewed instability in the global economy."[1] With this came a renewed focus on the prosperity and safety of the Asia-Pacific region, leading to emphasis in the 2011 NSS on the importance of developing and maintaining bilateral relationships with the myriad of countries throughout the region in order to "build broader cooperation on areas of mutual interest."[2]

Practical analysis suggests the United States will face many challenges pursuing current NSS aspirations, particularly in the Asia-Pacific region of the world. In addition to its global economic significance, the Asia-Pacific region contains six of the world's largest militaries three of which possess nuclear weapons.[3] The 2010 Quadrennial Defense Review (QDR) highlights one particularly alarming challenge: "the lack of transparency and the nature of China's military development," specifically identifying the "large numbers of advanced medium-range ballistic and cruise missiles, new attack submarines equipped with advanced weapons, increasingly

---

[1] Barack Obama, *National Security Strategy* (Washington, D.C.: Government Printing Office, 2010), 32.

[2] Ibid., 42.

[3] International Institute for Strategic Studies, "The Military Balance 2012," *The Military Balance.* 112, no. 1; "Status of World Nuclear Forces," Federation of American Scientists (FAS), http://www.fas.org/programs/ssp/nukes/nuclearweapons/nukestatus.html (accessed August 28, 2012).

1

capable long-range air defense systems, electronic warfare and computer network attack capabilities, advanced fighter aircraft, and counter-space systems."[4]

In concert with the NSS, the 2011 National Military Strategy (NMS) further amplified concern "about the extent and strategic intent of China's military modernization, and its assertiveness in the Yellow Sea, East China Sea, and South China Sea."[5] President Barak Obama subsequently announced a shift in U.S. strategic interests in January 2012 to the Asia-Pacific region, prompted in part by the Budget Control Act of 2011 and the opportunity presented by the reduction in operational requirements to support the wars in Iraq and Afghanistan. Former Secretary of Defense (SECDEF) Leon Panetta consequently issued his strategic guidance to the Department of Defense (DOD) based on the President's strategic direction. While the administration ultimately aims to enhance America's relationship with China to secure the nation's vital economic and security interests in the Western Pacific and East Asia, the NMS points out the reality that "China's emergence as a regional power will have the potential to affect the U.S. economy and our security in a variety of ways."[6] Specifically, the SECDEF directed the Joint Force to "recalibrate its capabilities and make selective additional investments" to accomplish a myriad of modified operational missions.[7] Two of the more significant missions directed by the SECDEF have particular relevance to the U.S. Submarine Force (SUBFOR): the missions to "deter and defeat aggression" and to "project power despite anti-access/area denial

---

[4]U.S. Department of Defense, *Quadrennial Defense Review Report* (Washington, D.C.: Government Printing Office, 2010), 30,60.

[5]U.S. Department of Defense, *The National Military Strategy of the United States of America 2011: Redefining America's Military Leadership* (Washington, D.C. : Governement Printing Office, 2011), 41.

[6]Ibid., 2.

[7]Ibid., 4.

challenges."[8] The use of seapower in these critical mission areas to protect the American way of life is fundamental to the coordinated maritime strategy.[9]

Assessments and Proposals

Upon receiving the President's guidance, the SECDEF directed the Center for Strategic and International Studies (CSIS) to conduct an independent assessment of U.S. force posture in Asia. While the CSIS overwhelmingly concurred with the DOD's overall assessment, its fundamental finding, published in a 2012 study conducted by two senior analysts of the Asia-Pacific region, centered on the "lack [of] an operational framework to match [the] strategic imperative."[10] Based on the immediate nature of the challenges that CSIS identified, it recommended promptly addressing a number of realistic near-term steps.[11] Nevertheless, the policy and funding logjams between DOD and Congress continue, compounded by the fact that DOD has neither articulated "the strategy behind its force posture planning nor aligned the strategy with resources in a way that reflects current budget realities."[12]

Recent Chinese activity in the South China Sea and throughout the Pacific Rim illustrates the critical need for America to build up forces rapidly to address the emerging anti-access and area denial (A2/AD) threats in the Asia-Pacific, with the ultimate goal of shaping the operational

---

[8]U.S. Department of Defense, *Sustaining U.S. Global Leadereship: Priorities for 21st Century Defense* (Washington, D.C.: Government Printing Office, 2012), 4.

[9]U.S. Navy, *A Cooperative Strategy for 21st Century Warfare* (Washington D.C.: Government Printing Office, October 2007); U.S. Navy, *Naval Operations Concept 2010: Implementing the Maritime Strategy* (Washington D.C.: Government Printing Office, 2010).

[10]David Berteau and Michael Green, *U.S. Force Posture Strategy in the Asia Pacific Region: An Independent Assessment* (Washington, D.C.: Center for Strategic and International Studies, 2012), 3.

[11]Ibid., 3-4.

[12]Ibid., 4.

environment such that a conflict is never necessary.[13] Of note, another CSIS report identified that, "given the increased size and operational reach of attack submarines from China's People's Liberation Army Navy (PLAN), the U.S. Navy faces an imbalance in its own submarine fleet in the Asia-Pacific region. This imbalance will grow rapidly in the mid-2020s as DOD prepares to retire U.S. nuclear attack submarines at a rate twice that of new construction for replacements."[14]

Presently, neither joint doctrine nor service specific doctrine has officially defined the terms anti-access and area denial, both of which – although not new concepts – are relatively new terms in the DOD discourse on Asia-Pacific strategy and military operations. Because of their pertinence to this discussion as well as the relative newness of the terms, the following analysis requires a clear definition of the terms anti-access and area denial for consistent use throughout this paper. In 2003, the Center for Strategic and Budgetary Assessments (CBSA) issued a report that contained suitable definitions. It defined "anti-access" as any strategy aimed to "prevent U.S. forces entry into a theater of operation" and "area denial" as any operation aimed to "prevent [U.S. forces] freedom of action in the more narrow confines of the area under an enemy's direct control."[15] Although a more detailed definition specific to aerial, land, and sea components is possible and likely in the future, the general DOD acceptance of anti-access relating to the ability to deploy forces into an area of operations and area denial the ability to keep them there as long as desired provide sufficient definition for use in the following analysis.[16]

---

[13]Ibid., 5.

[14]Ibid., 21.

[15]Andrew Krepinevich, Barry Watts, and Robert Work, *Meeting the Anti-Access and Area-Denial Challenge* (Washington, D.C.: Center for Strategic and Budgetary Assessments, 2003), ii.

[16]U.S. Department of Defense, "Background Briefing on Air-Sea Battle by Defense Officials from the Pentagon," http://www.defense.gov/transcripts/transcript.aspx?transcript id=4923 (accessed October 20, 2012).

Seemingly, the U.S. Government and DOD are awaiting the approval of a suitable

operational concept to guide the execution of this strategic shift. In September 2009, Chief of

Naval Operations Admiral Gary Roughead and Air Force Chief of Staff General Norton Schwartz

signed a memorandum of agreement to initiate an effort by their Services to develop a new

operational concept known as "AirSea Battle."[17] The CBSA took the lead to develop the AirSea

Battle concept "to assess how U.S. power-projection capabilities can be preserved in the face of

the military challenges posed by China and Iran."[18] The CBSA's detailed report includes several

recommendations for initiatives to combat the multitude of associated challenges.[19] While each of

the proposed initiatives appears sound based solely on the anticipated threat, the analysis herein

demonstrates that implementation is unfeasible from a U.S. Submarine Force perspective,

especially given the shrinking Defense Budget.

The U.S. Submarine Force's Role

Regardless what operational concept DOD ultimately embraces to address the concerns

in the Asia-Pacific region, SUBFOR will fulfill the predominant role in at least two of the

highest-profile categories. Specifically, SUBFOR possesses unique and unparalleled capabilities

in the areas of anti-access and anti-submarine warfare (ASW). China recognizes this capability,

as indicated by an assessment conducted by the People's Liberation Army (PLA) in 2005 that

---

[17]Christopher P. Cavas and Vago Muradian, "New Program Could Redefine AF-Navy Joint Ops," *Air Force Times*, November 15, 2009. http://www.airforcetimes.com/news/2009/11/ airforce _ navy_ cooperation_111509w/ (accessed August 22, 2012).

[18]Andrew F. Krepinevich, *Why Airsea Battle?* (Washington, D.C.: Center for Strategic and Budgetary Assessments, 2010), viii.

[19]Specifically at the operational level, the CBSA provides 21 initiatives with multiple subcategories as outlined in Jan Van Tol et al., *Airsea Battle: A Point-of-Departure Operational Concept* (Center for Strategic and Budgetary Assessments, 2012), 81-91.

indicated it "believes that U.S. nuclear submarines are very quiet, and difficult to discover and counterattack; at the same time, [their] attack power is great, [and] must [be] restrain[ed]."[20]

Meanwhile, competition for resources in the post-Cold War era resulted in a steady decline in SUBFOR assets and capabilities. This contentious but arguably necessary reprioritization of DOD funds forced USN leaders to make difficult operational choices regarding SUBFOR size and capability – with obvious ramifications regarding the ability to support adoption of a new national strategy. In the meantime, Chinese analysts continued to develop "intimate familiarity" with the U.S., French, British, and Russian submarine force programs in their efforts to build a submarine force commensurate with their needs.[21] PLAN Rear Admiral Yang Yi's 2006 analysis of the SUBFOR, in which he concluded "China already exceeds [U.S. submarine production] five times over…18 [USN] submarines against 75 or more Chinese navy submarines is obviously not encouraging [from the U.S. perspective]," demonstrates China's obvious goal of outpacing potential competetors' submarine capabilities.[22] While Yang Yi's comments compare submarines and weapons systems with very different capabilities – U.S. fast attack submarines (SSN) to PLAN diesel electric submarines (SSK) – this assessment provides important insight into Chinese thinking with respect to submarine operations. The continuing decline of SUBFOR – in quantity if not quality – significantly increases the risk that America will lose undersea supremacy in the Western Pacific for the first time since World War II. If not addressed, this situation could significantly undermine the USN's ability to maintain security of the global commons in the Asia-Pacific region.

---

[20]Gabriel Collins et al., "Chinese Evaluations of the U.S. Navy Submarine Force," *Naval War College Review* 61, no. 1 (Winter 2008): 70.

[21]Andrew S. Erikson and Lyle J. Goldstein, "China's Future Nuclear Submarine Force: Insights from Chinese Writings," *Naval War College Review* 60, no. 1 (Winter 2007): 61.

[22]Collins et al., "Chinese Evaluations of the U.S. Navy Submarine Force," 81. The discussion here should be tempered with the fact that not all of the reported 75 submarines are (or would be) nuclear powered; however, their numbers alone represent a significant threat.

The current U.S. intent to shift its strategic focus to the Asia-Pacific region has given the relative capability of SUBFOR and the PLAN's submarine fleet renewed significance. This leads to the necessity to determine whether the SUBFOR, as currently configured and based on its projected future configuration, can contend with the increasing A2/AD and ASW capabilities of the PLAN's rapidly growing and evolving submarine force. China has unquestionably shifted its strategic and operational focus over the last few decades, particularly in the maritime environment. Meanwhile, American policy makers have sought to minimize – if not eliminate – the likelihood of any military conflict with Beijing. However, as Carl von Clausewitz puts it,

> We are not interested in generals who win victories without bloodshed. The fact that slaughter is a horrifying spectacle must make us take war more seriously, but not provide an excuse for gradually blunting our swords in the name of humanity. Sooner or later someone will come along with a sharp sword and hack off our arms.[23]

Thus, America must remain poised to respond efficiently and effectively to protect the country's interests abroad. Since the late 1980s, China has sought to position itself as a regional major power. In particular, China has renewed its focus on the undersea operational environment. One can readily find evidence of this focus. For example, former PLAN commander General Liu Huaqing argued,

> [I]n order to safeguard China's coast, resist possible foreign invasion, and defend our maritime rights and interests, it is only right and proper that China should attach great importance to developing its own navy, including 'emphatic' development of its submarine force.[24]

As U.S. analysts observe Liu's recommendations rapidly turning into reality, the situation warrants an analysis focused on the current and projected SUBFOR's operational capability to offset the expansion over the past decade of Chinese naval capabilities.

---

[23]Carl von Clausewitz, *On War*, ed. and trans. Michael Howard and Peter Paret (Princeton, N.J.: Princeton University Press, 1976), 260.

[24]Quoted in Bernard D. Cole, "China's Maritime Strategy," in *China's Future Nuclear Submarine Force*, ed. Andrew S. Erickson, et al. (Annapolis, MD: Naval Institute Press, 2007), 26.

METHODOLOGY

An examination of SUBFOR capabilities in relation to the Chinese submarine and ASW threat in the Asia-Pacific demonstrates that the shift in strategic focus to the Asia-Pacific incurs a currently unrecognized or, more likely, an unacknowledged operational requirement for an increase in the number and capabilities of submarines in the U.S. Pacific Fleet. A comparative analysis of the PLAN submarine force's A2/AD and ASW capabilities – both current and projected over the next decade – and SUBFOR's ability to counteract that threat – serves as the primary methodological tool to facilitate this analysis. This comparative analysis demonstrates that a distinct deficit in the SUBFOR operational capability required to support the new strategy not only presently exists, but also will continue to grow if the USG does not substantially increase projected SUBFOR numbers and capabilities.

The following comparative analysis includes both a qualitative and quantitative analysis of the PLAN's submerged threat. Quantitative analysis of the current and projected numbers of subsurface A2/AD and ASW platforms within the PLAN identifies and differentiates the types and quantities of the various platforms and their relative capabilities. However, this strictly quantitative assessment does not take into account qualitative differences between SUBFOR and the PLAN, like technological advancements, organizational structure, leadership, training, and proficiency. Therefore, the qualitative assessment highlights these primarily subjective factors, focusing on those that make the PLAN's submerged threat particularly significant. These include China's advances in submarine design across the range of submerged platforms, their ever-increasing procurement process, and the significant armament capability that each submarine class possesses – or will soon possess (particularly with respect to the A2/AD and ASW roles).

As a matter of realistic comparative analysis as well as to provide additional justification for the conclusions reached herein, the final section will consist of a hypothetical – yet completely realistic – case study. The case study will highlight the challenges SUBFOR could potentially incur in an attempt to conduct operational art in the current and projected situation in the Asia-Pacific given the growing imbalance in submarine capability between the United States and China. The ultimate Chinese goal of assimilating Taiwan back into the fold provides a realistic context for the hypothetical conflict in the Western Pacific that serves as the basis of the hypothetical case study. Hence, following the assessment of the current and projected PLAN submarine force, a conceivable scenario will outline the operational impact of SUBFOR.

Annual DOD reports to Congress, Office of Naval Intelligence (ONI) reports, and Stephen Saunders' *Jane's Fighting Ships* serve as main sources of baseline data underpinning the comparative analysis. The work of various experts on China and its navy supplements these sources. These include, to name a few, Bernard D. Cole's *The Great Wall at Sea*, John Wilson Lewis and Xue Litai's *China's Strategic Seapower*, as well as various works by the Naval War College's (NWC) China Maritime Studies Institute (CMSI). Breaking the analysis and assessments down systematically and logically results in three distinct areas of focus. The PLAN diesel submarine (SSK) fleet provides a robust capability to operate in the substantial littoral environment of the Western Pacific. Its nuclear fast attack (SSN) fleet's power projection operations and capabilities potentially indicate the disposition among China's leadership to expand their global maritime influence. Finally, China's nuclear ballistic missile (SSBN) force foreshadows the potential for a Cold War-like scenario in which the United States and China emerge as the leaders in a renewed bipolar global standoff.

Delimitations, necessary to keep the analysis within length constraints, include exclusion of potential coalition allies (e.g., Japan, Australia, etc.) from the analysis. While the U.S. Navy will continue to strive for the global maritime partnership that Admiral Mike Mullen referred to as "the 1,000 ship navy," complete dependence on this concept involves unacceptable levels of risk.[25] Many historical examples exist that demonstrate the potential ramifications of overreliance

---

[25]Admiral Mike Mullen, "Commentary: We Can't Do It Alone," *Honolulu Advertiser*,

on the presumption that any U.S. naval effort in the Asia-Pacific would include support of allied partners.[26] Further, the analysis will not account for the plethora of non-submarine ASW platforms in the U.S. Navy's arsenal. While the USN maintains assets such as Maritime Patrol Aircraft (MPA) (such as the P-3C Orion) and guided missile destroyers (DDG) and frigates (FFG) that contribute to ASW, their capabilities have atrophied in recent years. Richard Fisher of the International Assessment and Strategy Center observed in 2005 that

> [o]ver the last decade the U.S. had decided to mothball its Spruance class destroyers, perhaps one of the best ASW ships ever built. The Navy also ended the ASW mission of the S-3 Viking in 1998 and will not even replace this platform when it is withdrawn from service in about two years.[27]

While the non-submarine ASW platforms provide significant supplemental capabilities in an ASW scenario, the unique characteristics of the primary ASW platforms – the attack submarines (SSN) and guided missile submarines (SSGN) – warrant an analysis that focuses solely on the submarine world.[28] Further, these delimitations make sense given the distinct possibility that the mismatch between the America's and China's submarine forces has grown (and will continue to grow) to the point that non-submarine ASW platforms will not provide adequate capability to tip the balance in America's favor.

The following examination of the areas outlined above demonstrates the validity of this study's thesis. Strategically, the USG has directed a shift in focus of America's military to the

---

October 29, 2006.

[26]Many historical examples exist to substantiate this claim as recent as OIF. For the Pacific Theater maritime philosophy, many examples of the British and U.S. disagreements are highlighted in Walter R. Borneman, *The Admirals: Nimitz, Halsley, Leahy, and King - the Five-Star Admirals Who Won the War at Sea* (New York: Little, Brown, and Company, 2012).

[27]Richard Fisher Jr., "Developing US-Chinese Nuclear Naval Competition in Asia," International Assessment and Strategy Center, http://www.strategycenter.net/research/pubID.60/pub_detail.asp (accessed November 27, 2012).

[28]Although the present arsenal of non-submarine ASW platforms in the USN remain formidable, many sources and examples highlight the atrophy of ASW capabilities over the last few decades, primarily driven by the lack of funding due to the military focus in Southeast Asia.

Western Pacific Theater of Operation (WPTO).This study highlights one particular area of operational risk associated with that shift in focus, resulting from the demands it places on SUBFOR after years of China's PLAN submarine fleet growing in relative numbers and capability. Ultimately, the conclusions reached will prove that to meet the mandates required in shifting U.S. strategic focus to the Asia-Pacific region, the USG and DOD must reprioritize funds and resources to allow for an increase in current and projected SUBFOR capabilities.

BODY

Background

> The PLAN has a long and illustrious lineage. China's naval forces have evolved through several distinct stages.
> —Bernard D. Cole, *The Great Wall at Sea: China's Navy in the Twenty-First Century*

John Lewis Gaddis advocates the importance of "interpret[ing] the past for the purposes of the present with a view to managing the future," suggesting the utility of a brief historical overview prior to embarking on the detailed analysis.[29] One can trace China's naval heritage back well over a millennium with a genesis in the "Spring and Autumn period," when, as Sun-Tzu astutely observed, the frequency and complexity of warfare began to evolve dramatically.[30] This ultimately led to the first Chinese naval peak during the Song Dynasty in the thirteenth century, followed by collapse during the latter part of the Ming Dynasty (1368-1644). Although dormant for the last few centuries, the resurrection of Chinese naval presence during the mid-twentieth century has caused many speculations among strategists, who wonder whether the Chinese government plans to restore the formidable naval supremacy that the Chinese Empire once

---

[29]John Lewis Gaddis, *The Landscape of History: How Historians Map the Past* (New York, NY: Oxford University Press, Inc., 2002), 10-11.

[30]Roger T. Ames, *Sun-Tzu the Art of Warfare* (New York, NY: Ballantine Books, 1993), 3-4. The Spring and Autumn period encompasses the period of time between 771 and 403 B.C.

enjoyed.[31] A brief synopsis of the PLAN development and maturation over the last 60 years –

focusing on the growth and modernization of the PLAN submarine force during the last two

decades – provides an interpretation of the history to aid in managing the future. While outsiders

cannot know what certainty what goals or ambitions China may ultimately have for their growing

PLAN force, their unquestionable naval buildup over the last half-century begs the question.

Following the PLAN's rebirth in May of 1950 and subsequent invasion of Taiwan in the

summer of 1951 in an attempt to seize offshore islands occupied by the Kuomintang (KMT), the

PRC renewed its focus on building a formidable maritime power.[32] Subsequently, two broad

areas appear to have initially reinvigorated China's renewed motivation in the maritime domain:

unwanted foreign military presence and territorial claims – both of which apparently tie into

China's global economic aspirations throughout the Asia-Pacific region. The fact than more than

half of the world's total merchant shipping – particularly raw materials, including vast quantities

of petroleum products – passes through the straits of Malacca, Sunda, and Lombok and into the

South China Sea highlights the power that results from dominance of the Western Pacific

maritime domain.[33]

The U.S. military "occupation" of the Asia-Pacific region – a longstanding point of

friction in Beijing – began with President Harry S. Truman's June 1950 decision to send the U.S.

Seventh Fleet into the Taiwan Strait at the outset of the Korean War. American forces established

air and sea superiority in the Western Pacific in the region and has maintained it ever since – a

---

[31]For a comprehensive discussion of the rise and fall of the Chinese Navy, see Gang Deng, *Chinese Maritime Activities and Socioeconomic Development, C. 2100 B.C.-1900 A.D.* (Westport, Conn.: Greenwood Press, 1997).

[32]Jonathan I. Charney and J. R. V. Prescott, "Resolving Cross-Straight Relations between China and Taiwan," *The American Journal of International Law* 94, no. 3: 453-77.

[33]Sam Bateman, Joshua Ho, and Mathew Mathai, "Shipping Patterns in the Malacca and Singapore Straits: An Assessment of the Risks to Different Types of Vessel," *Contemporary Southeast Asia* 29, no. 2 (August 2007): 309-32.

fact that China recognizes but has so far lacked the ability to challenge. While China may not have overtly sought to drive America out of the Western Pacific, its leaders have never embraced the dominant presence of U.S. Forces in their backyard.[34] The two nations have found themselves in precarious situations on several occasions over the last few decades – however, neglecting the number of demonstrations in the region throughout the recent years, China has never directly threatened U.S. forces in the Asia-Pacific region. However, there is evidence that the tide may be on the brink of shifting with a possible future scenario involving PLAN dominance of the maritime environment around China in support of potential shift in balance of power with the United States.[35]

A number of disputed territorial integrity claims between Beijing and of its geographical neighbors add friction in the region and increase the operational significance of the Western Pacific maritime domain. These frequent and sometimes heated clashes contribute to the PRC's perceived necessity to build a formidable naval power. China's ongoing quarrel with Taiwan nominally takes center stage, but other territorial claims remain matters of dispute. For example, China's ongoing disputes include one with: Japan over the Diaoyu/Senkaku Islands; another with Vietnam over both the Paracel Islands and the Vietnamese maritime border; a longstanding struggle with Taiwan, the Philippines, Vietnam, Brunei, and Malaysia over the Spratly Islands; and a region-wide dispute over control of the of the South China Sea (SCS).[36]

---

[34]Bernard D. Cole, *The Great Wall at Sea: China's Navy in the Twenty-First Century*, Second ed. (Annapolis, MD: Naval Institute Press, 2010), 7-18.

[35]David Lai, "The United States and China in Power Transition," Strategic Studies Institute, U.S. Army War College, http://purl.fdlp.gov/GPO/gpo17692 (accessed December 7, 2012).

[36]Desmond Ball, *Trends in Military Acquisitions in the Asia-Pacific Region : Implications for Security and Prospects for Constraints and Controls* (Canberra, Australia: Strategic and Defence Studies Centre, Australian National University, 1993), 27-28.

The 1982 United Nations Convention on the Law of the Sea (UNCLOS), including subsequent ratifications, should have solved many of these issues, at least in theory. In reality, confusion involved with the establishment of areas such as the contiguous zone (CZ), the economic exclusion zone (EEZ), and the continental shelf (CS) have only exacerbated the problem.[37] Present conditions remain tenuous at best throughout the Asia-Pacific region, indicated by diplomatic and military moves like PRC legislation that went into effect in 2012 that allowed Chinese police to board and seize control of ships that enter their claimed territorial waters. Such measures only increase the already significant volatility in the region.[38] The ever-festering dispute over economic interests, maritime control, and territorial claims could potentially lead to an unwanted and unpredictable escalation in regional turmoil. Given the fact that open access to Western Pacific maritime shipping lanes, along with various ongoing territorial disputes directly relate to vital U.S. national interests, any escalation could lead to American intervention.

These factors, combined with the rapid economic growth of the PRC over the last decade highlight the significance of China's intentions for its increasingly powerful navy. In particular, one wonders how China plans to employ the increasingly modernized PLAN submarine force – and whether SUBFOR possesses the operational capacity to encounter the threat that it might represent. Some may view the premise that the PLAN submarine force poses a potential threat unjustifiable; however, many analysts have come to this conclusion after detailed analysis of Chinese literature regarding its strategic aims and the PLAN's role at achieving them. For

[37]Chapter 2 of Cole, *The Great Wall at Sea.* provides a concise overview of the UNCLOS challenges as well as the historical maritime claim evolution of the countries throughout the Asia-Pacific region. For a detailed discussion of the key battlegound areas of the EEZs throughout the world, see James Kraska, *Maritime Power and the Law of the Sea: Expeditionary Operations in World Politics* (Oxford; New York, N.Y.: Oxford University Press, 2011).

[38]Matthew Bigg, "ASEAN Chief Voices Alarm at China Plan to Board Ships in Disputed Waters," *Reuters*, November 30, 2012. http://www.reuters.com/article/2012/11/30/us-china-seas-idUSBRE8AT01B20 121130 (accessed November 30, 2012).

example, Chinese strategy experts John Wilson Lewis and Xue Litai wrote in 1994 a comprehensive analysis of PRC strategy since the late 1980s in which they concluded that Beijing is systematically shifting from a coastal defense (*jinhai fangyu*) strategy to an offshore defense (*jinjang fangyu*) strategy. This offshore defense strategy involves an extension in China's defensive perimeter to a range of 200 to 400 nautical miles (nm) from the shores of Chinese claimed territory. With a long-term vision in mind, Beijing has openly affirmed intentions to shift to a global, blue-water navy (*yuanyang haijun*) by 2050.[39] As seen in Figure 1, this maritime territory is well within the first- and second island chains, which are home to vital U.S. national assets including the 7th Fleet headquarters in Yokosuka, Japan and the Naval Submarine Base in Guam.

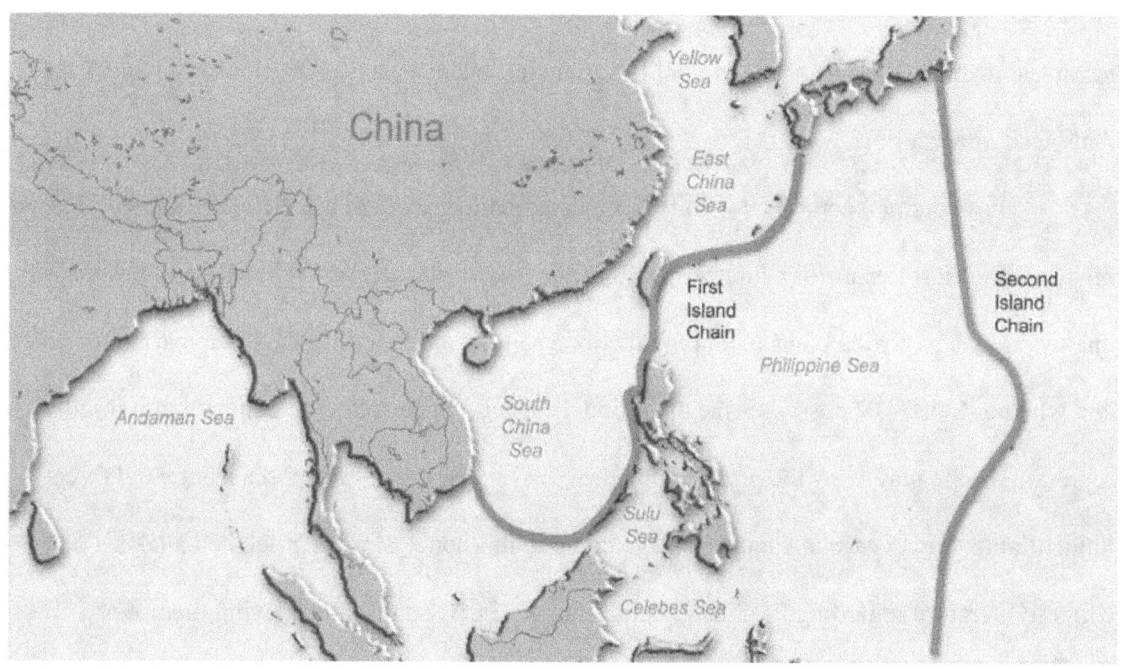

Figure 1. First and Second Island Chains

[39]John Wilson Lewis and Xue Litai, *China's Strategic Seapower: The Politics of Force Modernization in the Nuclear Age* (Stanford, CA: Stanford University Press, 1994), 229-30; Paul H.B. Godwin, "China's Emerging Military Doctrine: A Role for Nuclear Submarines?" in *China's Future Nuclear Submarine Force*, ed. Andrew S. Erickson, et al. (Annapolis, MD: Naval Institute Press, 2007), 43-58 provides a concise update to Lewis and Litai's 1994 conclusions, presenting a more recent view of Chinese strategy and doctrine with respect to the PLAN submarine force.

Source: ONI Report, *The People's Liberation Army Navy: A Modern Navy with Chinese Characteristics*

In its naval strategy, China mainly follows the fundamental principles described by American naval theorist Alfred Thayer Mahan, such as the idea that seaborne trade serves as an integral part of national power, and the ability to conduct seaborne trade requires control of the sea.[40] This makes sense for the increasingly economically powerful Beijing and, assuming relations between China and the United States remain cordial, the potential exists for a healthy and prosperous relationship for all parties throughout the region. On the other hand, China's ongoing regional disputes, economic ambition, and buildup of naval power all highlight the importance of SUBFOR readiness to contend with potential PLAN aggression. The Clausewitzian adage that "if the enemy is to be coerced you must put him in a situation that is even more unpleasant then the one you call on him to make" highlights SUBFOR's operational predicament.[41] SUBFOR retains responsibility to counter the PLAN submarine threat, but lacks clear dominance over this increasingly large and powerful force, posing significant risk to U.S. national interests.

The Chinese SSK Wolfpack

Although Mao envisioned a Chinese undersea force and promised that China would build a nuclear submarine "if it took 10,000 years," the development of the PLAN submarine force began with conventional diesel-electric submarines.[42] China's ostensible SSK proliferation, particularly in the vast littoral areas of the Asia-Pacific region, presents growing strategic and

---

[40] A. T. Mahan, *The Influence of Sea Power Upon History 1660-1783* (New York: Dover Publications, 1987), 29-89.

[41] Clausewitz, *On War*, 77.

[42] Quoted in William S. Murray, "An Overview of the Plan Submarine Force," in *China's Future Nuclear Submarine Force*, ed. Andrew S. Erickson, et al. (Annapolis, MD: Naval Institute Press, 2007), 69.

operational concerns for the security and protection of the global commons – concerns that SUBFOR retains an unparalleled capacity to address. Although restricted in their power projection capabilities because of the operational limitations of diesel engines, evolving SSK designs have maximized technology's potential, making these submarines an increasingly formidable weapon – one that, at a minimum, can significantly disrupt other nations' freedom of movement in the Western Pacific. The favorable bathymetric areas of the East China Sea, Yellow Sea, and – most notably based on the number of strategic chokepoints – the South China Sea (SCS) areas are optimal for SSK operations.[43] Additionally, operations in the high contact density shallow water of the Asia-Pacific region's littoral environments increase the acoustic challenges associated with locating and identifying submerged SSKs.[44]

The Soviet Union helped China create its submarine force, selling the PLAN Soviet designed *Whiskey-* and *Romeo*-class SSKs in the mid-1950s. With the assistance of documentation provided by the USSR and some reverse ingenuity, China succeeded in semi-indigenous production Romeo derivatives and – with the addition of modern equipment from Western nations – the improved *Romeo* (known in the West as the *Ming*-class) – SSKs in the early 1960s. While only an estimated nineteen of these antiquated designs remain in service, they still present a significant threat.[45] Although stereotypically noisy and near the end of their service

---

[43]Cole, *The Great Wall at Sea*, 23. The SCS area contains the Straits of Malacca, Sunda, and Lumbok as well as the number of SLOCs throughout the Spratly Islands.

[44]For a complete discription of the complex environmental characteristics associated with submarine operations in a littoral evnvironment, including the effects on submarine acoustic detections, see John R. Benedict, "The Unraveling and Revitalization of U.S. Navy Antisubmarine Warfare," *Naval War College Review* 58, no. 2 (Spring 2005): 92-120.

[45]Stephen Saunders, *Jane's Fighting Ships 2011-2012* (Coulsdon, UK: IHS Global Limited, 2011), 132; James C. Bussert and Bruce A. Elleman, *People's Liberation Army Navy: Combat Systems Technology, 1949-2010* (Annapolis, MD: Naval Institute Press, 2011), 63-64. The exact numbers and specifics associated with the Soviet S- and W-class submarines sold and delivered to the PLAN are uncertain; however, the point is insignificant since none remain in service.

lives, continued operation of these World War II era submarines complicates the ASW and AD picture in the vast Chinese littoral environment. Regardless of their sub-standard acoustic performance and outdated design, these SSKs remain capable of performing a number of operationally significant missions – such as laying mines, enforcing exclusion zones, or targeting merchant ships – all of which represent a daunting ASW challenge for even the most capable of submarine forces. Recent modernization efforts have only increased the threat posed by China's SSKs.

In 1993, Beijing purchased four *Kilo*-class SSKs from Moscow and subsequently contracted to acquire an additional eight in 2002.[46] The *Kilo* acquisitions combined with additional advanced military technology assistance from Russia resulted in the development of the first truly indigenous PLAN diesel submarine – the Type 039 *Song*-class – and, more recently, the Type 041 *Yuan*-class SSK. The latter is of particular interest as not only did it catch many Western analysts by surprise, but also because the likelihood exists that China fitted the *Yuan* with the advanced air independent propulsion (AIP) system. This feature would enable the *Yuan* to operate in a more SSN-like hunter-killer style because the AIP would enable the Yuan to conduct extended submerged operations, remaining submerged and undetected for longer periods (as compared to a normal SSK which nominally must snorkel to recharge its batteries about once a day).[47] Proper operation of the more modern, quieter SSKs adds an additional layer of stealth, extended reach, increased tactical capabilities, and, when employed in their nominal operating environment, makes them a formidable A2/AD and ASW challenge.

Regardless of the significant progress in advancement of their conventional submarine force, the PLAN cannot overcome the fundamental limitations of diesel-electric submarines.

---

[46]Saunders, *Jane's Fighting Ships 2011-2012*, 134.

[47]Richard Scott, "Conventional Wisdom," *Jane's Defense Weekly 2011*, April 7, 2011. https://janes.ihs.com.lumen.cgsccarl.com/CustomPages/Janes/DisplayPage.aspx?DocType=News &ItemId=+++1186616&Pubabbrev=JDW (accessed January 23, 2013).

While SSKs are intrinsically quiet and therefore challenging to detect and track, even incorporation of AIP cannot overcome the inherent slow-speed operation and range limitations of diesel boats. However, the characteristics of the geographical areas in the Western Pacific surrounding the Chinese coastline – combined with PLANs advancement in A2/AD, ASW, or anti-surface warfare (ASUW) weapons – provides a number of significant advantages for the Chinese SSK fleet, particularly when analyzing PLAN weapons capabilities.

The torpedo remains the traditional weapon most often associated with submarine warfare, although modern submarines possess a wide variety of weapon capabilities. A superficial glance may suggest that the torpedo no longer poses a serious threat in twenty-first century warfare, particularly when one considers the fact that the last torpedo launch in a time of war occurred over three decades ago.[48] However, on closer inspection the torpedo still served as a simple yet effective weapon, and one that the Chinese have worked to improve as technology has evolved. The numerous narrow straits throughout the Asia-Pacific region, combined with China's modernization of its torpedo technology that has enabled the PLAN to employ torpedoes commensurate with the MK 48 U.S. design make China's variants capable weapons for use in AD, ASW, and ASUW roles.[49] The Yu-6, the PLAN's most advanced indigenous torpedo, possesses a respectable set of capabilities. It is wire-guided, has both active and passive sensors, and is both acoustic- and wake-homing. The Yu-6 has a reported range between twenty-six and fifty kilometers.[50] China purchased two other advanced torpedoes from Russia for use both in their *Kilos* and in their SSNs: the Russian-built TEST 96 wake-homing torpedo, and the TEST

---

[48]Damian Housman, "Lessons of Naval Warfare," *National Review* July 23, 1982: 894-96.

[49]For an overview of the PLAN torpedo design and evolution (including comparable USSR or US equivalent variants), see Table 21 of Bussert and Elleman, *People's Liberation Army Navy: Combat Systems Technology, 1949-2010*, 74.

[50]"Yu-6 Heavyweight Torpedo," Military Periscope, https://www.militaryperiscope.com. lumen.cgsccarl.com/weapons/minetorp/torpedo/w0007747.html (accessed November 29, 2012).

71MKE hydro-acoustic homing, wire guided torpedo. Each has a range of up to twenty-five kilometers.[51] While all of the torpedoes in the PLAN arsenal remain inferior to the U.S. MK-48 Advanced Capability (ADCAP) or the Common Broadband Advanced Sonar System (CBASS) designs, they constitute a formidable threat, particularly within the multitude of narrow, strategic chokepoints throughout the Pacific Rim.[52]

To supplement the torpedo armament – thus improving the operational reach of the SSKs – China can arm them with a myriad of both Chinese and foreign-built anti-ship cruise missiles (ASCM). The thirteen *Song*-class and up to four *Yuan*-class SSKs observers believe China now possess reportedly carry the domestically produced, forty-two kilometer range YJ-82 ASCM with the potential of carrying the longer (but yet undetermined) range ASCM – NATO code name CH-SS-NX-13 – once development and testing are complete.[53] Even more alarming from the ASCM perspective, the newly received *Kilos* obtained from Russia are outfitted with the deadly 180 kilometer range submerged torpedo tube- and vertical-launched Russian SS-N-27B/Sizzler (a Novator Klub series) ASCM.[54] This particular ASCM leads to particular concern because of its classification "…as part of the best family of cruise missiles in the world and, in the opinion of some, able to defeat the U.S. Aegis air and missile defense system that is central to the defense of

---

[51]"Test 71MKE Torpedo," Military Periscope, https://www.militaryperiscope.com/weapons/minetorp/torpedo/w0006155.html (accessed December 4, 2012).

[52]For a basic overview of the latest MK-48 heavyweight torpedo designs, see "MK-48 Heavyweight Torpedo," U.S. Navy Fact File, http://www.navy.mil/navydata/fact_display.asp?cid=2100&tid=950&ct=2 (accessed January 24, 2013).

[53]IHS Jane's, "Enter the Dragon: Inside China's New Model Navy," *Jane's Navy International*, April 20, 2011. https://janes.ihs.com.lumen.cgsccarl.com/CustomPages/Janes/DisplayPage.aspx ?DocType=News&ItemId=+++1208610&Pubabbrev=JNI (accessed November 27, 2011).

[54]U.S. Department of Defense, *Annual Report to Congress: Military and Security Developments Involving the People's Republic of China 2012* (Washington, D.C.: Government Printing Office, 2012), 21-23.

carrier strike groups."[55] Further, once the Chinese successfully developed capable ASCMs, they took the next logical step for the PLAN submarine force – for SSKs and SSNs alike – the development of commensurate land-attack missiles similar to the American-made Tomahawk land attack missile (TLAM). Combining China's torpedo advances, its short- and medium-range ballistic missile capabilities, and the effectiveness of these systems in the classical roles in which the PLAN will most likely employ its submerged vessels, one can only conclude that the PLAN SSK fleet represents a significant operational challenge to the U.S. Navy – particularly SUBFOR.

Including the delivery of the twelfth and final *Kilo* to China in 2006, the total conventional submerged compliment of the PLAN submarine force amounts to approximately forty-eight vessels – a number that will continue to grow in the near term.[56] In addition to the aforementioned SSKs, reports indicate that China will soon add a new, presently undesignated SSK to its conventional fleet that is one-third larger than the *Yuan* and could potentially carry China's first solid-fueled SLBM – the 1,500 to 2,000 km range DF-21D.[57] The ever-increasing number of diesel submarines in Beijing's arsenal adds significantly to the PLAN's AD and ASW capabilities. Additionally, the expansion and technological improvement of the PLAN SSK force has allowed the Chinese SSKs to operate increasingly far from the Chinese coast, which enhances their A2 capabilities. Although inferior to U.S. submarines in most respects, the total number of

---

[55]Eric A. McVadon, "China's Maturing Navy," in *China's Nuclear Submarine Force*, ed. Andrew S. Erickson, et al. (Annapolis, MD: Naval Institute Press, 2007), 9. The Aegis Ballistic Missile Defense (BMD) system is the sea-based element of the U.S. BMDS carried aboard *Ticonderoga* (CG--47) Class cruisers and *Arleigh Burke* (DDG-51) Class destroyers designed to incercept and destroy SRBMs and MRBMs; "Russia to Deliver SS-N-27 to China," *China Defence Today*, April 29, 2005. http://www.sinodefence.com/news/2005/news29-04-05.asp (accessed November 1, 2012). The SS-N-27B initially makes a subsonic flight to the target area, followed by a supersonic, sea-skimming evasive attack to the target.

[56]Saunders, *Jane's Fighting Ships 2011-2012*, 134.

[57]Ted Parsons, "Images of Mystery Chinese Sub Prompt More Questions Than Answers," *Jane's Defense Weekly 2011*, May 26, 2011. https://janes.ihs.com.lumen.cgsccarl.com/ CustomPages/Janes/DisplayPage.aspx?DocType=News&ItemId=+++1187032&Pubabbrev=JDW (accessed January 24, 2013).

SSKs that the PLAN could potentially employ in a conflict would definitely combine the increasing capability of China's submarine fleet with a significant numerical strength, or mass – a fundamental principle of war, and one that has particular significance in a maritime environment. For example if massed against a decisive point, such as a U.S. Carrier Strike Group (CSG) even the qualitatively inferior PLAN could still pose a significant operational threat to U.S. naval forces.[58]

Operational Implications of the PLAN Ballistic Missile Submarine Force

The Chinese SSK fleet represents merely the tip of the iceberg when evaluating the range of PLAN submerged threats. Developments stemming from Beijing's aspirations to develop a reputable "strategic" ballistic missile nuclear submarine force underscore the necessity to analyze any additional operational impacts on SUBFOR. As indicated above, a myriad of issues initially prevented China from achieving nuclear development at the same pace as Rickover's Nuclear Navy. These issues stemmed primarily from the political, social, and economic turmoil that plagued the PRC throughout the second half of the twentieth century.[59] Nevertheless, significant technological advancements combined with the improved military relations with Russia and unprecedented availability of open-source references on pressurized nuclear water reactor designs and operations have put China on the fast track to develop an SSBN force similar to that possessed by the Kremlin throughout the Cold War.[60] As the United States and Soviet Union

---

[58]Office of Naval Intelligence, "The People's Liberation Army Navy: A Modern Navy with Chinese Characteristics," http://www.oni.navy.mil/Intelligence_Community/docs/china_army_navy.pdf (accessed October 10, 2012).

[59]Lewis and Litai, *China's Strategic Seapower*, 1-20.

[60]Robert G. Loewenthal, "Cold War Insights into China's New Ballistic-Missile Submarine Fleet," in *China's Future Nuclear Submarine Force*, ed. Andrew S. Erickson, et al. (Annapolis, MD: Naval Institute Press, 2007), 286-303; Shawn Cappellano-Sarver, "Naval Implications of China's Nuclear Power Development," in *China's Future Nuclear Submarine Force*, ed. Andrew S. Erickson, et al. (Annapolis, MD: Naval Institute Press, 1997), 114-34; Richard D. Fisher Jr., "The Impact of Foreign Technology on China's Submarine Force and

realized in the mid-1960s, the PRC appears to understand that submarine launched nuclear

ballistic missiles (SLBMs) remain the most survivable leg of the nuclear triad. Hence, it appears

China has used the lessons learned during the Cold War to develop the capability to project power

globally using nuclear SLBMs, contributing to its apparent strategic aim of rising to the level of a

regional – if not global – hegemon.

China's first ballistic missile submarine – the *Xia* design of the early 1980s – remains

incapable of accomplishing the strategic deterrent mission and, although she still occasionally

goes to sea, she has yet to make – and likely will never make, in Professor William S. Murray's

words – a "credible deterrent patrol."[61] While equipped with the relatively capable 1,600 nautical

mile (nm) range JL-1 SLBM, it took six years following *Xia*'s commissioning to achieve a

satisfactory missile launch.[62] Because of the significant failures *Xia* experienced (and continues to

experience) as well as the Cold War focus on Moscow's SLBM program throughout that period,

it follows that minimal USG concerns existed with respect to the potential strategic and

operational implications of the nascent PLAN SSBN program. However, China's recent revival

and evolution of this seemingly dormant program warrant reassessment of the initial assumptions

and reevaluation of the potential risk associated with continued United States presence in the

Western Pacific.

The second generation PLAN SSBN, known in the West as the *Jin*-class, became

operational in 2007. A projected class of six *Jins*, capable of carrying up to twelve of the proven

4,320 nm JL-2 SLBMs, could conceivably provide the continuous at sea presence of a formidable

---

Operations," in *China's Future Nuclear Submarine Force*, ed. Andrew S. Erickson, et al. (Annapolis, MD: Naval Institute Press, 2007), 135-61.

[61]Murray, "An Overview of the Plan Submarine Force," 64.

[62]Saunders, *Jane's Fighting Ships 2011-2012*, 130.

ballistic missile force and could realistically achieve full operational capability by 2016.[63]

Chinese President Hu Jintao has stated that he considers this additional leg of Beijing's submarine arsenal part of "[b]uilding strong national defense and powerful armed forces that are commensurate with China's international standing." Further, Jintao indicated that the requirement to "meet the needs of its security and development interests is a strategic task of China's modernization drive."[64] Seemingly, this would complete a nuclear triad for the PRC reasonably proportionate with U.S. capabilities, particularly given the proposed SUBFOR SSBN cuts over the next decade.

This development begs the question just how far Chinese nuclear ballistic missile submarine aspirations extend as they look to the future. Since it appears that China plans to develop a ballistic missile submarine force capable of continuous strategic deterrence, prudence calls for an analysis of SUBFOR operational capability to meet this potential future threat. One wonders whether the United States and China could emerge as the competing parties in a second bipolar, Cold War-like scenario similar to the one that plagued the world for the better half of the twentieth century. If so, this warrants an assessment of the likelihood and feasibility of a U.S. 'barrier strategy' similar to that used against the Soviet Union throughout the Cold War. Many U.S. analysts speculate on the potential operating patterns of a PLAN SSBN force, debating whether Beijing would assume a bastion strategy within the protective confines of the Bohai and Yellow Seas or would take the more ambitious approach of deploying into the blue water depths

---

[63]Murray, "An Overview of the Plan Submarine Force," 64; "China Advances Missile Program," *The Washington Times*, June 21, 2005. http://www.washingtontimes.com/news/2005/jun/21/20050621-102521-5027r/ (accessed September 23, 2012); Saunders, *Jane's Fighting Ships 2011-2012*, 130; Jim Wolf, "Update 2 - China Submarines Soon to Carry Nuclear Weapons, US Draft Report Says," *Reuters*, November 8, 2012. http://www.reuters.com/article/2012/11/08/china-usa-military-idUSL1 E8M80YW20121108 (accessed November 8, 2012).

[64]Quoted in Jim Wolf, "Update 2 - China Submarines Soon to Carry Nuclear Weapons, US Draft Report Says," *Reuters*, November 8, 2012, http://www.reuters.com/article/2012/11/08/china-usa-military-idUSL1 E8M80YW20121108 (accessed November 8, 2012).

of the Pacific.[65] The challenges associated with operating in the complex acoustic shallow water environment of the sanctuaries would seem to indicate that the latter provides a more viable long-term option, thus imposing significant operational requirements on SUBFOR.

PLAN Control of Sea Lines of Communication and Power Projection with Nuclear Fast Attack Submarines

While the Chinese SSK and SSBN forces provide genuine operational concerns for SUBFOR, including the PLAN nuclear fast attack fleet in the equation adds both additional complexity and operational requirements. As China continues to grow and evolve economically, so does its necessity (whether real or perceived) to project power in order to control Beijing's sea lines of communication (SLOC).[66] Strategically as well as operationally, this is a natural and necessary evolution for the growing future of the PRC. Although protecting the SLOCs is an inherent right for any country, the underlying aspirations associated with China's evident advances to accomplish this with a SSN force appear debatable when looking at recent real world events. The PRC's clear examples of the planned extension of their power projection out to – at a minimum – the second island chain are undeniable.[67] The development of its nuclear fast attack fleet stands at the forefront of China's power projection intentions and the role of the PLAN submarine force in achieving them. Realizing the inherent advantages of nuclear power over

---

[65]Toshi Yoshihara, "U.S. Ballistic Missile Defense & China's Undersea Deterrent," in *China's Future Nuclear Submarine Force*, ed. Andrew S. Erickson, et al. (Annapolis, MD: Naval Institute Press, 2007), 342-43.

[66]A good discussion of the potential SSN role in SLOC protection can be found in James Patton, "Cold War SSN Operations: Lessons for Understanding Chinese Naval Development," in *China's Future Nuclear Submarine Force*, ed. Andrew S. Erickson, et al. (Annapolis, MD: Naval Institute Press, 2007), 278-81.Of note, it is unclear whether SLOC protection is the ultimate goal or merely an excuse to build a formidable SSN force. In either case, the potential exists for the buildup to turn into a self-perpetuating phenomenon.

[67]See Alexander Huang, "The Chinese Navy's Offshore Active Defense Strategy: Conceptualization and Implications," *Naval War College Review* 47, no. 3: 16-18. for a detailed discussion of the bounds of the first- and second-island chains.

diesel electric power, China is rapidly capitalizing on a number of opportunities to build a formidable SSN force – a force that has the capability of rivaling that of American SSNs within the next decade.

The advantages of harnessing the energy of nuclear power over the conventional diesel electric propulsion system provide a number of additional capabilities for the PLAN submarine force. Following the 1993 *Yin Hi* incident, China elected to capitalize further on this capability. PRC high command leadership desired a "capable and superior nuclear attack submarine that could protect China's shipping in distant seas," particularly after considering that their numbers of nuclear attack submarines were "insufficient and the capabilities backward....Thus, they [were] inadequate to cope with the requirements of the new strategic situation."[68] As with challenges in the SSBN world, the PLAN experienced similar challenges in initial SSN development. Reconciling many of the issues that originally plagued its SSN force, as with the SSBN force, the PLAN continues to make significant advances in building a respectable SSN force commensurate with meeting China's needs.

Although originally completed in 1974, the first Chinese SSN – the Type 091 *Han*-class – did not achieve "fully operational" status until 1980.[69] While they remain noisy, outdated, and aging, three *Han*-class SSNs linger in service and continue to contribute to the offensive capability and striking power of the PLAN nuclear submarine fleet. Sino-Russian relations

---

[68]Quoted in Andrew S. Erickson and Lyle J. Goldstein, "China's Future Nuclear Submarine Force: Insights from Chinese Writings," in *China's Future Nuclear Submarine Force*, ed. Andrew S. Erickson, et al. (Annapolis, MD: Naval Institute Press, 2007), 184-85; Erickson et. al. derived this quote from Lin Changsheng, "The Combat Power of China's Nuclear Submarines," *World Aerospace Digest*, no. 103 (September 2004): n13 noting that Lin is a former Taiwanese military officer who spent time in the U.S. on a research fellowship.; Additionally, see "Saudis Board a Chinese Ship in Search for Chemical Arms," *The New York Times*, August 28, 1993. http://www.nytimes.com/1993/08/28/world/saudis-board-a-chinese-ship-in-search-for-chemical-arms.html (accessed November 8, 2012) for information on the Saudi boarding of *Yin He* in search for chemical arms.

[69]Saunders, *Jane's Fighting Ships 2011-2012*, 132.

combined with foreign technological assistance resulted in the development of the newer Type 093 *Shang*-class SSNs that are reportedly similar in performance to and derived from the second generation Russian *Victor IIIs*.[70] Although reports vary as to the end strength of the *Shang*, estimates indicate that the PLAN currently possesses somewhere between three and six in service, and has the strong potential to field up to five more of an improved and modified design – the *Shang* Type 095.[71]

The lingering question regarding the PLAN SSN fleet remains a matter of its ability to support the A2/AD mission and its corresponding power projection capability. This includes the related and significant ASW and ASUW threat and the SSN's contribution to China's inherent ability to maintain routine control of SLOCs. While China has identified the latter as the ultimate goal or the asserted mission of its SSN fleet, events throughout the past few decades suggest the former may play a significant if unspoken role in Beijing's ultimate intent for its ongoing PLAN expansion. The covert and clandestine nature inherent to submarine operations potentially adds a layer of ambiguity to this particular analysis; however, investigations and commonalities among the recent real world events provide useful insight to add insight to the potential motives of China.

The first known incident involving a PLAN SSN and a U.S. naval vessel took place in 1994, when the USS *Kitty Hawk* battle group detected a *Han*-class submarine shadowing it in the Sea of Japan from October 27 – 30. This incident led to a tense standoff when the battle group commander ordered a U.S. S-3B MPA to track the *Han*, prompting the PLA to send J-6 fighters

---

[70]Ibid., 131; Office of Naval Intelligence, *Worldwide Submarine Challenges* (Washington D.C.: Government Printing Office, February 2007), 23. As a matter of comparison, both sources generally regard the Russian *Victor III* design to be acoustically similar to the earlier SSN-688 *Los Angeles*-class submarines.

[71]Fisher Jr., "The Impact of Foreign Technology on China's Submarine Force and Operations," 147; Saunders, *Jane's Fighting Ships 2011-2012*, 131.

to intercept the American ASW aircraft.[72] Operating in international waters, following the United

Nations Convention on the Law of the Sea (UNCLOS) regulations, U.S. Navy forces often locate

foreign military warships. Common practice, even if merely for the training value alone,

inevitably results in tracking these vessels. The U.S. S-3Bs violated no international laws and

displayed no hostile intent toward the *Han*. However, the PLAN chose in this case to interpret

tracking as an aggressive act (ironically, since this merely involved a response to a PLAN

submarine tracking the U.S. naval force), and it heightened the tensions by sending fighters to

interact with the MPA. However, the incident ended with no shots fired.

A little over a decade later, a Japanese anti-submarine patrol aircraft (P-3C) identified

and tracked a *Han* as it made a submerged incursion through the Ishigaki Strait into Japanese

territorial waters on November 10, 2004.[73] While the *Han* incident with the *Kitty Hawk* was

legally justified (on both sides) as it unfolded in international waters, the latter was clearly in

violation of the UNCLOS. In the Japanese territorial water case, the *Han* clearly failed "to

navigate on the surface and to show [her] flag."[74] In diplomatic language, Beijing attempted to

dismiss the incident using a plethora of excuses such as navigational error.[75] Many of the reasons

---

[72]"Type 091 Han Class," GlobalSecurity.org, http://www.globalsecurity.org/military/ world/china/type-91.htm (accessed December 4, 2012).

[73]Miyoshi Masahiro, "The Submerged Passage of a Submarine through the Territorial Sea - the Incident of a Chinese Atomic-Powered Submarine," *Singapore Yearbook of International Law* 10 YSBIL: 243; Reiji Yoshida, "Beijing Says Tech Glitch Led to Sub Intrusion," *The Japan Times Online*, November 17, 2004. http://www.japantimes.co.jp/ text/nn20041117a1.html (accessed September 23, 2012).

[74]United Nations Conference on the Law of the Sea, 3d, *United Nations Convention on the Law of the Sea*, A/CONF. 62/122 (n.p.: 1982).

[75]For a more in-depth discussion on the *Han* incident as well as the legal and international implications, see Peter A. Dutton, "International Law and the November 2004 "Han Incident", in *China's Future Nuclear Submarine Force*, ed. Andrew S. Erickson, et al. (Annapolis, MD: Naval Institute Press, 2007), 162-81; Masahiro, "The Submerged Passage of a Submarine through the Territorial Sea - the Incident of a Chinese Atomic-Powered Submarine."; Yoshida, "Beijing Says Tech Glitch Led to Sub Intrusion," *Japan Times*, November 17, 2004. http://www.japantimes. co.jp/text/ nn20041117a1.html (accessed September 23, 2012).

the PLAN offered for its actions seemed plausible; however, its tendency to change the story or use the same excuses repeatedly for pushing the limits of the UNCLOS cause most to question the validity of China's official explanations. Later interactions with PLAN vessels reinforced other nations' suspicions regarding China's intentions.

A third incident involving a Chinese *Song* "stalking" the *Kitty Hawk* Strike Group as it conducted operations in international waters near Okinawa a couple of years later potentially indicates different aspirations. In the *Song* case – again, initially dismissed by the Chinese Foreign Ministry – the PLAN SSK surfaced within torpedo range of the carrier.[76] Although a myriad of internal questions arose in the 2006 *Kitty Hawk* incident, as in the 1994 case no UNCLOS laws were broken on either side. Nevertheless, two interactions of PLAN SSNs beyond the first island chain – combined with Beijing's overtly dismissive posture – justify concern among U.S. naval planners regarding PLAN naval activities and intentions. Additionally, the innately covert nature of submarine operations begs the question of what other questionable PLAN SSN operations could have occurred but gone unnoticed.

While the technology and capabilities of the PLAN submarine force continue to improve, the Chinese submarine fleet still has several key shortcomings that merit examination. For example, the PLAN SSN's power projection capability includes the ability to geo-locate and track American carrier strike groups (CSG) or expeditionary strike group (ESG) – two of America's most often and effectively used means of establishing a regional presence or conducting a show of force. Actual tracking and integration within the PLAN SSN community, however, requires an

---

[76]Bill Gertz, "China Sub Stalked U.S. Fleet," *The Washington Times*, November 13, 2006. http://www. washingtontimes.com/news/2006/nov/13/20061113-121539-3317r/ (accessed November 7, 2011); "Chinese Sub Came Close to U.S. Ships," CBS News, http://www.cbsnews. com/2100-202_162-2179694.html (accessed November 7, 2012); David Axe, "China's Overhyped Sub Threat," *The Diplomat*, October 20, 2011. http://thediplomat.com/2011/10/20/china%E2%80%99s-overhyped-submarine-threat/ (accessed November 7, 2011). Of note, it is likely more plausible that - rather than "surfacing" - the PLAN Song "broached" or "inadvertently surfaced" in the vicinity of the carrier strike group.

extensive command, control, and communication (C3) system. A few inherent challenges presently limit Beijing's ability to optimize the C3 within the PLAN submarine fleet. Multiple lines of command exist in the PLAN hierarchy, making it organizationally unprepared to meet the needs of modern warfare. Beijing's determination to maintain centralized versus decentralized command over its navy – the latter requiring a better-trained officer corps and a culture of trust between government and military that currently does not exist – will continue to present an additional obstacle to PLAN effectiveness.[77] Although the PLAN submarine force's C3 presently remains a weak spot, it would be unwise to ignore the possibility that China might recognize and resolve these challenges, enabling the PLAN to reach its full potential to conduct A2/AD and other missions.

Whether power projection, control of SLOCs, an A2/AD threat, or an ASW/ASUW threat, Beijing's apparent strategic aims and the growing submarine prowess it had developed in recent years present a significant operational concern for SUBFOR. China has left open the possibility that it has no offensive or territorial ambitions in its actions and stated strategic goals. Further, China's lack of overseas bases provides justification for the PLAN's development of a formidable blue-water SSN force with the operational reach needed to protect China's vital national interests. However, China's lack of transparency in its strategic goals and actions, and the trends in its behavior during recent real world events leaves its long-term strategic goals and the purpose of its rapidly growing operational capability – particularly in its submarine fleet – open to question. In fact, China's careful study of Great Britain's nuclear submarine force – particularly its deliberate implementation of British lessons learned from the British Navy's SSN

---

[77]For information on the evolution and challenges associated with C3 within the PLAN submarine force, see Garth Heckler, Ed Francis, and James Mulvenon, "C3 in the Chinese Submarine Fleet," in *China's Future Nuclear Submarine Force*, ed. Andrew S. Erickson, et al. (Annapolis, MD: Naval Institute Press, 2007), 213-28.

deployment during the Falkland's War – provides clear evidence of its intentions to develop a worldwide SSN presence.[78]

U.S. Submarine Force Projections and Analysis

This section provides an overview of SUBFOR projections for comparison with the anticipated PLAN submarine force in an objective attempt to analyze the relative force projections. The current posture of the U.S. Submarine Force consists of fifty-five attack submarines (SSN) – thirty-one in the Pacific and twenty-four in the Atlantic, four guided missile attack submarines (SSGN) – two in each theater, and 14 ballistic missile submarines (SSBN) – eight in the Pacific and six in the Atlantic.[79] For the future SSN compliment, the proposed procurement of *Virginia*-class submarines continues at a rate of, on average, two per year through FY2018 with nine hulls delivered between FY2014 and FY2018.[80] In parallel, the Navy is retiring a number of the older *Los Angeles*-class submarines. The result yields the present 30-year plan forecasting a projected low for the fast-attack force of forty-three hulls by the year 2028.[81] With the looming financial cuts to the DOD budget and resultant potential changes in the defense strategy, this number could go even lower.[82] To put a perspective on this number, the planned compliment under the Reagan-era plan for a 600 ships was 100 SSNs. This number dropped to

[78]Erickson and Goldstein, "China's Future Nuclear Submarine Force: Insights from Chinese Writings," 187.

[79]"United States Submarine Force Organization," Commander, Submarine Force Atlantic, http://www.sublant.navy.mil/ (accessed February 21, 2013).

[80]Ronald O'Rourke, *Navy Virginia (SSN-774) Class Attack Submarine Procurement: Background and Issues for Congress* (Washington, D.C.: Congressional Research Service, Report for Congress, RL32418, April 2, 2012), 5.

[81]Christopher P. Cavas, "30-Year Plan Has Fleet Size at About 300 Ships," *Navy Times*, March 28, 2012. http://www.navytimes.com/news/2012/03/defense-30-year-navy-plan-fleet-size-about-300-ships-032812 (accessed November 25, 2012).

[82]Craig Whitlock, "Budget Cutting Spurs Hagel to Order Pentagon Review of Year-Old Strategy," *Washington Post*, March 19,2013, 11.

eighty under the George H. W. Bush Administration's Base Force plan of 1991-1992 and fell

further to forty-five to fifty five SSNs following the Clinton Administration's 1993 Bottom Up

Review (BUR).[83] Over a decade after the Joint Chiefs of Staff (JCS) study of December 1999 (in

response to the QDR of 1997) one cannot help but wonder about the validity of the following

conclusion in 2013 and beyond:

> that a force structure below 55 SSNs in the 2015 and 62 [SSNs] in the 2025 time frame
> would leave the CINC's [the regional military commanders in-chief] with insufficient
> capability to respond to urgent crucial demands without gapping other requirements of
> higher national interest. Additionally, this force structure [55 SSNs in 2015 and 62 in
> 2025] would be sufficient to meet the modeled war fighting requirements.[84]

Considering the further planned reductions in the SSN fleet, this assessment seems particularly

dated and in need of reevaluation.

In addition to the SSN requirements, SUBFOR must also account for the operational

demands of America's most survivable element of the nuclear triad. Maintaining the legacy

dating of over half a century back to the *George Washington*-class SSBN, the current *Ohio*-class

SSBN has greatly contributed to the over 4,000 U.S. strategic deterrent patrols since 1960.[85] As

the *Ohio*-class SSBNs are nearing their end of service lives, design and development are

underway for twelve of the next generation ballistic missile submarines, or SSBN(X)s, to replace

the fourteen *Ohio*-class SSBNs presently in service.[86] Strategic discussions aside, the operational

impact to SUBFOR is negligible from a numbers standpoint as well as the inherent nature of

---

[83]O'Rourke, *Navy Virginia (SSN-774) Class Attack Submarine Procurement: Background and Issues for Congress*, 19; Secretary of Defense Les Aspin, *Report on the Bottom-up Review* (Washington D.C.: Department of Defense, October 1993), 55-57.

[84]O'Rourke, *Navy Virginia (SSN-774) Class Attack Submarine Procurement: Background and Issues for Congress*, 19.

[85]Vice Admiral John M. Richardson, "Primus in Pace," Commander Submarine Forces, http://comsubfor-usn.blogspot.com/2012/07/primus-in-pace.html (accessed November 1, 2012).

[86]Ronald O'Rourke, *Navy SSBN(X) Ballistic Missile Submarine Program: Background and Issues for Congress* (Congressional Research Service, Report for Congress, RL41129, March 19, 2010), 1.

SSBN operations, which consists entirely of a focus on strategic deterrence.[87] Depending on the timeline for SSBN(X) procurement, the remaining hull-life of the retired *Ohio*-class SSBNs and funding decisions, the potential exists to convert more replaced SSBNs to SSGNs, (the first four *Ohio*-class SSBNs underwent this conversion), although to date, DOD has announced no plans to do so.

Some proponents suggest the United States should invest in a SSK fleet to meet the littoral challenges of the Western Pacific; however, this also appears merely an option, with no active planning along these lines taking place.[88] Hence, the focus remains the operational SUBFOR SSN/SSGN force and the impact of the foregoing issues on its efficacy and relative capability with respect to America's strategic concerns. The two broad areas of significance for this particular analysis revolve around evaluation of the impacts with respect to the PLAN SSBN force and the PLAN SSN/SSK force. As demonstrated above, historical precedent and current assessments of likely PLAN submarine force employment indicate that the potential exists for the Chinese to maintain a forward deployment of their SSBN force into the open ocean environment of the Pacific. Hence, it seems plausible for the United States to respond with a barrier strategy similar to that employed against the Soviet Union throughout the Cold War. As President John F. Kennedy proposed in 1961,

> the principal measures of protection should be provided by the capability to attack prior to launch… [therefore] the United States should strive to achieve and maintain an effective and integrated sea surveillance system that permits detection and tracking of surface ships and submarines operating within missile-launching range of the North American continent; and should improve its related anti-submarine capability.[89]

---

[87]For a discussion on the strategic justification to reduce the nuclear SLBM presence, see ibid. and Ronald O'Rourke, *Navy Trident Submarine Conversion (SSGN) Program: Background and Issues for Congress* (Congressional Research Service, Report for Congress, RS20017, May 22, 2008).

[88]As an example, see Milan Vego, "The Right Submarine for Lurking in the Littorals," *U.S. Naval Institute Proceedings* 136, no. 6: 16-21.

[89]Quoted in Owen R. Cote, "The Third Battle: Innovation in the U.S. Navy's Silent Cold

As this thinking and implementation contributed to prevention of a nuclear attack throughout the Cold War, one can see the logic of a similar strategy vis-à-vis China. The SUBFOR fast attack fleet is the most efficient platform in the military's arsenal to accomplish this task. Assuming the PLAN succeeds in building a new class of submarines consisting initially of six operational *Jins*, a reasonable operating pattern suggests four of the six would maintain a forward presence with the remaining two in port undergoing routine maintenance. In a scenario such as this, the operational requirement of SUBFOR to provide a reasonable capability to attack prior to launch would be twenty submarines – or, at a minimum, five to ten if one assumes the PLAN will conduct a limited number of PLAN SSBN patrols.[90] In comparison with the projected SUBFOR numbers, this alone could potentially require the dedicated effort of as much as half of America's fast attack submarine inventory.

Evaluation of SSN numbers with respect to the PLAN SSN/SSK force is much more subjective than comparison to the PLAN SSBN fleet. Although much detail regarding the challenges America faced when dealing with the threat of the former Soviet Union remains classified, one can make reasonable estimates regarding the potential effect on future SUBFOR operations as America deals with the newly emerging Chinese PLAN threat from the myriad of articles and books written on its Cold War corollary.[91] SUBFOR SSNs will continue to maintain a forward presence throughout the globe to protect the national interests of the United States – particularly in the Western Pacific. The range of SSN missions across the globe – such as

---

War Struggle with Soviet Submarines," *Naval War College Newport Papers*, no. 16: 20.

[90]The SUBFOR estimations are based on the analysis and conclusions drawn by Christopher McConnaughy, "China's Nuclear Undersea Deterrent," in *China's Future Nuclear Submarine Force*, ed. Andrew S. Erickson, et al. (Annapolis, MD: Naval Institute Press, 2007), 97.

[91]While remaining at an unclassified level, many inferences with respect to submarine operations in the SSN community can be derived from Christopher Drew and Sherry Sontag, *Blind Man's Bluff* (New York, NY: Perseus Book Group, 1998).

intelligence, surveillance, and reconnaissance (ISR), TLAM strike, ASW, ASUW, and Combat Search and Rescue (CSAR) to name a few – combined with the PLAN SSN and SSK proliferation suggest the planned number of SSNs in the SUBFOR arsenal may be inadequate to meet the operational demands.

The intent is not to suggest SUBFOR will accomplish this challenge in isolation. The remainder of the USN and other elements of the DOD bring unique capabilities to the region that will help to mitigate the A2/AD and ASW threat posed by China. Additionally, U.S. allies in the Asia-Pacific region – all of whom have concerns similar to those of the United States– provide assets and support to maintain the global common SLOCs throughout the region. This joint force and coalition support is invaluable; however, as Captain (ret) James H. Patton, former Commanding Officer of the USS *Pargo* (SSN-650) attests, "the U.S. Army may have embraced the enlistment mantra of 'An Army of One,' but in a very real sense, a modern SSN comes close to being 'A Battle Group of One.'"[92] Thus, when it comes to the potential challenges the United States faces in the Western Pacific, nothing compares to the irreplaceable benefits offered by the most powerful submarine force in the world. The PLAN's continued pace of closing the quality gap while outpacing the SUBFOR in the quantity of submarine forces inevitably begs the question at what point the risk reaches an unacceptable level, and how the United States can avoid that situation.

SUBFOR Operational Capacity to React to an Invasion of Taiwan

The PRC claims that Taiwan is an inalienable part of China and has reserved the right to use force to unify Taiwan with the mainland if Taiwan declares independence, if Taiwan is occupied by a foreign country, if it acquires nuclear weapons, or if Taiwan indefinitely refuses the peaceful settlement of cross-Strait reunification through negotiation. U.S. policy opposes any use of force to settle this dispute.
— Report to Congress Pursuant to Public Law 106-113

---

[92]Patton, "Cold War SSN Operations: Lessons for Understanding Chinese Naval Development," 280.

The future of U.S. international relations with China – particularly concerning the potential for a future military standoff or more violent conflict – remains unknown and unpredictable. Where one falls on the topic of the determinants and future direction of the U.S.-China relationship primarily depends on the influence of various international relations schools of thought. While a number of proponents suggest – as most would like to believe – that the Sino-American relationship will prosper in the future, the United States would be unwise to fail to prepare for other scenarios. Prudence therefore – predominantly from a military perspective – dictates an analysis of more threatening possibilities. While liberal optimists show minimal concern about future conflict with a rising China, emphasizing instead factors like mutually beneficial trade relationships, Professor Aaron L. Friedberg emphasizes the more pessimistic realist view that China's rising power will inevitably result in conflict.[93] One expert who represents this school of thought, John J. Mearsheimer, has predicted, "over the next few decades, the United States and China are likely to engage in intense security competition with considerable potential for war."[94] These philosophies are not solely limited to the U.S. point of view. In 2000, Colonel Qiao Liang and Colonel Wang Xiangsui (two senior colonels in the PLA) released a rather disturbing publication entitled *Unrestricted Warfare: China's Master Plan to Destroy America*. This book reveals an attitude in which China views America as the "enemy" and describes the many means that China can employ to overcome the U.S. technological advantage to achieve a military victory and replace America as global hegemon.[95]

Given the reasonable likelihood of some form of future military conflict with China – a scenario that analysts and military personnel on both sides of the Pacific increasingly anticipate,

[93] Aaron L. Friedburg, "The Future of U.S.-China Relations: Is Conflict Inevitable?," *International Security* 30, no. 2 (Fall 2005): 17-21.

[94] John J. Mearsheimer, "China's Unpeaceful Rise," *Current History*, April 2006: 160.

[95] Liang Qiao, Al Santoli, and Xiangsui Wang, *Unrestricted Warfare : China's Master Plan to Destroy America* (Panama City, Panama: Pan American Pub., 2000).

plan, and prepare for –a hypothetical case study serves as a useful counterfactual form of analysis. In particular, such a case study illustrates the potential risk the United States would face in a future conflict with China – particularly following planned reductions of SUBFOR. As an example, numerous indications throughout the latter half of the 20th century indicate that the CCP continues to embrace Mao Zedong's goal of restoration of Taiwan into the greater Chinese fold as "part of [the] great cause of unifying China."[96] Numerous incidents over the last six decades indicate Beijing's continued resolve to conquer Taipei. Washington, on the other hand, remains firmly committed to the protection of Taiwan as an independent state.[97] As the PLAN submarine force continues its rapid advancement in all facets, it possesses the ability to mass a wolfpack from Quindago to Yulin to supplement a naval and amphibious offensive, or provide naval support to a joint operation against Taiwan if such a scenario as this were to unfold. Hence, this hypothetical case study examines the potential role the PLAN submarine force may play in this scenario as well as the imaginable ramifications if SUBFOR is ill equipped to respond.

A number of schools of thought exist on the ways and means Beijing would likely use to recapture Taipei.[98] While the most plausible scenario suggests using coercive measures – such as a ballistic missile attack or a naval blockade – the analysis herein addresses one particularly dangerous course of action that China could undertake. The potentially most deadly form of war over Taiwan would involve a PRC amphibious invasion of Taiwan that would require U.S. air support, augmented with both surface and subsurface naval support. Historically, whenever China has undertaken an act of aggression against Taiwan, the United States – at a minimum – has

---

[96]Quoted in Cole, *The Great Wall at Sea*, 8.

[97]*Taiwan Relations Act of 1979*, Public Law 96-8, 96th Cong. (April 10, 1979).

[98]As an example, Piers M. Wood and Charles D. Ferguson, "How China Might Invade Taiwan," *Naval War College Review* 54, no. 4 (Autumn 2001): 55-68 hypothesizes a phased invasion hopping across the Quemoy (Kinmen) islands to the Peng Hu islands to Taiwan's west coast.

deployed one or more CSGs to the region as a show of force. A successful amphibious assault requires a number of ingredients, including air and maritime superiority. A CSG deployed to the vicinity of the Taiwan Strait would make China's attainment of air and maritime superiority unlikely.[99]

Dr. James Kraska, the Howard S. Levie Chair of Operational Law at the U.S. Naval War College (NWC) described in a 2010 article entitled "How the United States Lost the Naval War of 2015" a plausible sequence of events that illustrates how such a conflict could unfold.[100] Knowing that the expected U.S. response to any hostilities towards Taiwan would initially include a CSG show of force with a corresponding establishment of local air and maritime superiority, the PLA would make negation of U.S. CSG assets its main priority, with the sinking of a carrier the ideal outcome. The PLA would rely on land-based solid-propelled MRBMs to accomplish this goal – specifically, the "carrier killer" DF-21D that it used to sink the forward deployed carrier, USS *George Washington*, moored in Yokosuka, Japan to the bottom of the East China Sea during a recent war game exercise.[101]

[99]For a counter argument of the infeasibility of China's invasion of Taiwan, see Michael O'Hanlon, "Why China Cannot Conquer Taiwan," *International Security* 25, no. 2 (Fall 2000): 51-86.

[100]James Kraska, "How the United States Lost the Naval War of 2015," *Orbis* Winter 2010: 35-45; For information on Dr. Kraska's credentials validating use of his article as a referent source, see "Faculty - James Kraska, JACG, CDR, USN," U.S. Naval War College, http://www. usnwc.edu/Academics/Faculty/James-Kraska,-CDR.aspx (accessed March 28, 2013).

[101]Although the PRC claims use of the DF-21D is specifically for self-defense, "PLA 'Sinks' US Carrier in DF-21D Missile Test in Gobi," *Want China Times*, January 23, 2013. http://www. wantchinatimes.com /news-subclass-cnt.aspx?cid=1101&MainCatID=11&id= 20130123000112 (accessed January 24, 2013) shows a recent war-game scenario that may suggest otherwise.

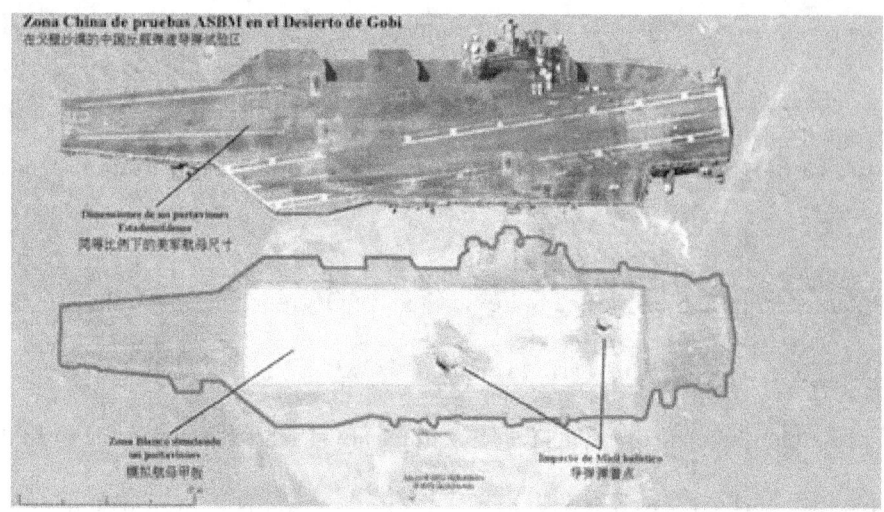

Figure 2. PLAN war-gaming sinking of a U.S. Carrier with a DF-21D

Source: *Want China Times* (http://www.wantchinatimes.com/news-subclass-cnt.aspx?cid =1101&MainCatID=11&i%20d=20130123000112)

Upon a successful carrier strike and sinking, an Operations Report 3 (OPREP-3) would disseminate this news to the Commander, Pacific Fleet (COMPACFLT), the SECDEF, and the White House within minutes. As President Bill Clinton said during his 1993 visit to the aircraft carrier USS *Theodore Roosevelt*, "When word of crisis breaks out in Washington, it's no accident the first question that comes to everyone's lips is: where is the nearest carrier?"[102] Next, COMPACFLT would contact the SECDEF to provide the information the President required to decide how to respond. With the inventory of carriers in the U.S. arsenal at an all-time low, and CSGs spread thinly around the globe, the COMPACFLT could potentially have bad news for the SECDEF: his closest flat top, the USS *Ronald Reagan*, moored in San Diego, California (6,000 nm away) could require up to two weeks to arrive in theater.

Meanwhile, with the predominant naval threat neutralized, the PLAN would then array its fleet – including the modified Russian-built CV *Liaoning*, an assortment of *Sovremeny*-, *Luda*-,

---

[102]"The Carriers," America's Navy, http://www.navy.mil/navydata/ships/carriers/cv-why.asp (accessed January 30, 2013).

Luhu-, *Luhai-*, *Luyang-*, *Luyang* II-, and *Luzhou-*class destroyers– in a cordon around Taiwan. In concert with the surface fleet, the PLAN SSKs would mass in the advantageous terrain of the littoral areas of the Taiwan Strait, while the PLAN SSNs established a forward perimeter that extended beyond the second island chain to provide the A2 for the Pacific Rim. This deployment of the PLAN destroyers, SSNs, and SSKs would create a powerful barrier capable of neutralizing remaining U.S. surface threats in the area. America's inability to reinforce its maritime assets in the area quickly would provide the PLAN sufficient time to lay sophisticated magnetic and acoustic influence mines throughout the Taiwan Strait, creating another defensive element to its cordon that the USN possesses limited ability to counter. Thus, the PLAN would achieve air and maritime superiority in the region surrounding Taiwan in short order. With the PLAN firmly postured to intercept reinforcements, the PLA could then conduct an amphibious assault on the mainland of Taiwan with little concern for U.S. interference.

Upon the U.S. SECDEF's notification that the USN will require at least two weeks to move a CBG in theater, providing the PLA significant time to establish a defense in depth, he would seek other options. The SECDEF would inquire about the status of the DDGs and FFGs in theater, while reports continued to reach the Joint Staff and U.S. Pacific Command (USPACOM) indicating that the PLAN arsenal of SS-N-27B/Sizzlers has rendered the remains of the surface fleet throughout the Western Pacific combat ineffective. Frantically searching for a feasible course of action, the SECDEF would soon learn from COMPACFLT that, much like after the Japanese attack on Pearl Harbor, submarines made up the majority of remaining naval assets unaffected by the attack. However, he would be dismayed to learn that even these – forward deployed to Submarine Squadron 15 (CSS-15) in Guam, consist of only three vessels, each of which possesses a limited capacity, if any, to respond. With one undergoing extensive modernization and unavailable for an operational assignment, while the other two – USS *Houston* (SSN-713) and USS *Oklahoma City* (SSN-723) – as well as USS *Michigan* (SSGN-727)

40

deployed in the Western Pacific Area of Responsibility (AOR) awaiting orders on the rules of engagement (ROE), the USN's few available naval assets would provide no immediate operational capability.

The SECDEF's analysis of the situation would lead to very limited military options that he could present to POTUS. The three fast attack submarines, although tactically and technologically superior to the PLAN fleet, suffer from a sever deficit in total armament; therefore, engagement with the PLAN would carry a high level of risk. The other logical option – conducting a TLAM strike to take out critical PLA C3 capabilities and vital PLA resources – would reveal the locations of the few remaining U.S. forces in theater to PLA intelligence analysts. This would require a limited TLAM strike to preserve the secrecy of site locations and improve their odds of survival, simultaneously limiting the damage the strike could cause to the PLA. In this scenario, the PLA, supported by a very capable and numerous PLAN fleet, would probably retain the capability to conduct a successful amphibious assault, leading to dire consequences for Taiwan.

CONCLUSIONS AND RECOMMENDATIONS

Nuclear attack subs are the most worthwhile weapons investments because they are the most survivable weapons platforms… During a regional conflict, [U.S.] nuclear attack submarines are the first in and last out.
—Chinese Naval Analyst Qian Jin, "Chinese Evaluations of the U.S. Submarine Force"

The above analysis demonstrates the relative – and growing – deficit between SUBFOR and the PLAN submarine force. Regardless of this deficit, SUBFOR remains tasked with a myriad of global operational commitments. Hence, a continued reduction in SUBFOR assets incurs a potentially excessive level of risk at the operational level if SUBFOR cannot meet the demands required by national security priorities. The shift in America's focus from the predominantly land-based warfare experienced in the Middle East throughout the last decade to the maritime challenges of the Pacific Theater highlights the relevance of this this critical assessment of the required SUBFOR operational capabilities. While SUBFOR has been reasonably postured to meet the operational demands of the last few decades, the current trend may prove disastrous for the long-term health of SUBFOR. Decisions made today could lead to irreparable impacts in the future, particularly when considering that advancements in submarine construction prevent rapid construction of a submarine force to meet immediate unanticipated demands. The sophisticated nature of submarine design and technology, requiring more stringent controls and oversight on submarine construction compared to historical times, result in a nominal sixty-month timeline to build a *Virginia*-class submarine.[103]

While the hypothetical scenario presented may appear unrealistic or unsubstantiated if taken strictly at face value, at a minimum it highlights a need for further analysis. The reality of such a conflict would a significantly more complex and interrelated series of events. Additionally, a variety of plausible scenarios exist, including many lower-intensity events such as mine laying and subsequent damage to U.S. assets, or cyber-attacks to infiltrate the critical infrastructure of the U.S. military – which could affect the strategic goals in the Pacific. China's lack of transparency, particularly in military affairs, adds an additional layer to the unknown. Accounting for such factors such as globalization and the economic interdependence that China enjoys on the worldwide stage, it seems contrary to the PRC's best interest to risk an international conflict – at least at the present time. However, the rapid buildup of the PLAN military forces with the simultaneous reduction in U.S. forces may jeopardize SUBFOR's capacity to meet the Commander in Chief's strategic focus in the shift to the Western Pacific.

President Obama's 2012 *Sustaining U.S. Global Leadership: Priorities for 21ˢᵗ Century Defense* as well as the 2011 NSS direct the DOD to shift its focus to the Asia-Pacific region, an area where SUBFOR will play a significant role in combatting the A2/AD concerns. Recent

---

[103]O'Rourke, *Navy Virginia (SSN-774) Class Attack Submarine Procurement: Background and Issues for Congress*, 6.

discussions on Capitol Hill suggest that the looming fiscal battles have prompted the SECDEF to order a reassessment of the current defense strategy to accommodate the tighter budgets. Although the Chairman of the Joint Chiefs of Staff (CJCS) predicts a change in the defense strategy, it is unclear how significant or fundamental this change could be.[104] Assuming the United States will remain a global power vice shifting to a regional power, addressing the A2/AD concerns in the Western Pacific remains a cornerstone of this strategy.

The continuing resolutions, budgetary constraints, and sequestration that plague the USG force hard decisions at all levels for the near future – from Congress to the DOD to the U.S. Navy. Current U.S. Navy funding under a Continuing Resolution has already caused budget shortfalls in SUBFOR, affecting its ability to meet operational commitments. The sequestration that went into effect in March 2013 resulted in significant additional budget reductions that have exacerbated the problem. Many potential short- and ultimately long-term ramifications of these budgetary constraints on SUBFOR exist, including – just to name two examples – cancellation of several SSN deployments and deferring emergent repairs (such as USS *Miami* (SSN-755) and USS *Montpelier* (SSN-765)).[105] An ongoing reassessment of the defense strategy requires the DOD to relook its assumptions and correspondingly adjust ambitions to match abilities.[106]

While it may result in a scaled down version, the reassessed defense strategy will likely attempt to meet the goals of the current defense strategy and will still require the full range of

---

[104]Whitlock, "Budget Cutting Spurs Hagel to Order Pentagon Review of Year-Old Strategy."

[105]*Direction Regarding the Continuing Resolution and Sequestration,* (Washington, D.C., January 25, 2013); Naval Sea Systems Command Public Affairs, "Navy Provides Updated Cost Estimate for USS Miami Repair," America's Navy, http://www.navy.mil/submit/ display.asp?story_id=69153 (accessed February 22, 2013); U.S.Fleet Forces Command Public Affairs, "USS Montpelier and USS San Jacinto Pierside," America's Navy, http://www.navy.mil/ submit/display.asp?story_id=70139 (accessed February 22, 2013).

[106]Whitlock, "Budget Cutting Spurs Hagel to Order Pentagon Review of Year-Old Strategy," 11.

military capabilities across the joint services. However, since financial concerns serve as the predominant drivers of this reassessment, one should recognize that an investment in SUBFOR provides an optimum way to match abilities with ambitions, particularly in the Asia-Pacific region. When viewed from the perspective of cost effectiveness, investment in SUBFOR provides an efficient way to meet defense demands. As an example, for the price of one *Gerald R. Ford*-class CVN, the USN could procure six *Virginia*-class SSNs. Similarly, for the cost of one *Zumwalt*-class DDG, SUBFOR could procure two *Virginia*-class SSNs.[107] The CVN and DDG are invaluable national defense assets with unique capabilities that undoubtedly make them critical to the USN in its support to the operational and strategic goals of the defense strategy. However, submarines provide equally unique and critical capabilities, making essential a reevaluation of SUBFOR projections with respect to Defense Department spending as the DOD makes difficult budgetary decisions in the near future.

China has made no effort to hide the rise of the PLAN submarine force and it shows no sign of slowing down. Although debates will continue regarding China's true intentions, a more numerous and more capable PLAN submarine force, equates to higher the risk for the United States and its allies. Economically, the United States plays an indisputably significant role in maintaining the sea lines of communication and mitigating the A2/AD and ASW concerns in the Western Pacific. SUBFOR plays a vital role in meeting these operational demands, but the current trend in end-strength reductions translates to risk to SUBFOR's operational capability.

---

[107]The average cost for the first three CVN-78s is $12.5 billion dollars as outlined in Ronald O'Rourke, *Navy Ford (CVN-78) Class Aircraft Carrier Program: Background and Issues for Congress* (Washington, D.C. : Congressional Research Service, Report for Congress RS20643, December 10, 2012), 4-5; The average costs for the first three DDG-1000s is $3.8 billion as outlined in Ronald O'Rourke, *Navy DDG-51 and DDG-1000 Destroyer Programs: Background and Issues for Congress* (Washington, D. C.: Congressional Research Service, Report for Congress RL32109, February 14, 2013), 6; As a matter of comparison, the nominal SSN-774 Class submarine procurement cost is $2 billion as discussed in Ronald O'Rourke, *Navy Virginia (SSN-774) Class Attack Submarine Procurement: Background and Issues for Congress*, 6.

Although one cannot predict the future numbers or capabilities of SUBFOR assets with a high degree of precision, the analysis herein highlights that a projected end-strength of forty-three hulls by 2030 – or less depending on financial constraints – will severely limit SUBFOR's ability to meet the operational demands of the future.

BIBLIOGRAPHY

Admiral Mike Mullen. "Commentary: We Can't Do It Alone." *Honolulu Advertisor*, October 29, 2006.

Ames, Roger T. *Sun-Tzu the Art of Warfare*. New York, NY: Ballantine Books, 1993.

Axe, David. "China's Overhyped Sub Threat." *The Diplomat*. October 20, 2011. http://the diplomat.com/2011/10/20/ china%E2%80%99s-overhyped-submarine-threat/ (accessed November 7, 2011).

Ball, Desmond. *Trends in Military Acquisitions in the Asia-Pacific Region : Implications for Security and Prospects for Constraints and Controls*. Canberra, Australia: Strategic and Defence Studies Centre, Australian National University, 1993.

Bateman, Sam, Joshua Ho, and Mathew Mathai. "Shipping Patterns in the Malacca and Singapore Straits: An Assessment of the Risks to Different Types of Vessel." *Contemporary Southeast Asia* 29, no. 2 (August 2007): 309-32.

Benedict, John R. "The Unraveling and Revitalization of U.S. Navy Antisubmarine Warfare." *Naval War College Review* 58, no. 2 (Spring 2005): 92-120.

Berteau, David, and Michael Green. *U.S. Force Posture Strategy in the Asia Pacific Region: An Independent Assessment* Washington, D.C.: Center for Strategic and International Studies, 2012.

Bigg, Matthew. "ASEAN Chief Voices Alarm at China Plan to Board Ships in Disputed Waters." *Reuters*. November 30, 2012. http://www.reuters.com/article/2012/11/30/us-china-seas-idUSBRE8AT01B 20121130 (accessed November 30, 2012).

Borneman, Walter R. *The Admirals: Nimitz, Halsley, Leahy, and King - the Five-Star Admirals Who Won the War at Sea*. New York: Little, Brown, and Company, 2012.

Bussert, James C., and Bruce A. Elleman. *People's Liberation Army Navy: Combat Systems Technology, 1949-2010*. Annapolis, MD: Naval Institute Press, 2011.

Cappellano-Sarver, Shawn. "Naval Implications of China's Nuclear Power Development." In *China's Future Nuclear Submarine Force*, edited by Andrew S. Erickson, Lyle J. Goldstein, William S. Murray and Andrew R. Wilson. Annapolis, MD: Naval Institute Press, 1997.

"The Carriers." America's Navy. http://www.navy.mil/navydata/ships/carriers/cv-why.asp (accessed January 30, 2013).

Cavas, Christopher P. "30-Year Plan Has Fleet Size at About 300 Ships." *Navy Times*. March 28, 2012. http://www.navytimes.com/news/2012/03/defense-30-year-navy-plan-fleet-size-about-300-ships-032812 (accessed November 25, 2012).

Cavas, Christopher P., and Vago Muradian. "New Program Could Redefine AF-Navy Joint Ops." *Air Force Times*. November 15, 2009. http://www.airforcetimes.com/news/2009/11/ airforce_navy_ cooperation_111509w/ (accessed August 22, 2012).

Changsheng, Lin. "The Combat Power of China's Nuclear Submarines." *World Aerospace Digest*, no. 103 (September 2004): 30.

Charney, Jonathan I., and J. R. V. Prescott. "Resolving Cross-Straight Relations between China and Taiwan." *The American Journal of International Law* 94, no. 3: 453-77.

"China Advances Missile Program." *The Washington Times*. June 21, 2005. http://www.wash ingtontimes.com/ news/2005/jun/21/20050621-102521-5027r/ (accessed September 23, 2012).

"Chinese Sub Came Close to U.S. Ships." CBS News. http://www.cbsnews.com/2100-202_162-2179694.html (accessed November 7, 2012).

Clausewitz, Carl von. *On War*. Edited and Translated by Michael Howard and Peter Paret. Princeton, N.J.: Princeton University Press, 1976.

Cole, Bernard D. "China's Maritime Strategy." In *China's Future Nuclear Submarine Force*, edited by Andrew S. Erickson, Lyle J. Goldstein, William S. Murray and Andrew R. Wilson, 22-42. Annapolis, MD: Naval Institure Press, 2007.

———. *The Great Wall at Sea: China's Navy in the Twenty-First Century*. Second ed. Annapolis, MD: Naval Institute Press, 2010.

Collins, Gabriel, Andrew Erickson, Lyle Goldstein, and William Murray. "Chinese Evaluations of the U.S. Navy Submarine Force." *Naval War College Review* 61, no. 1 (Winter 2008): 68-86.

Cote, Owen R. "The Third Battle: Innovation in the U.S. Navy's Silent Cold War Struggle with Soviet Submarines." *Naval War College Newport Papers*, no. 16.

Deng, Gang. *Chinese Maritime Activities and Socioeconomic Development, C. 2100 B.C.-1900 A.D.* Westport, Conn.: Greenwood Press, 1997.

Drew, Christopher, and Sherry Sontag. *Blind Man's Bluff*. New York, NY: Perseus Book Group, 1998.

Dutton, Peter A. "International Law and the November 2004 "Han Incident." In *China's Future Nuclear Submarine Force*, edited by Andrew S. Erickson, Lyle J. Goldstein, William S. Murray and Andrew R. Wilson. Annapolis, MD: Naval Institute Press, 2007.

Erickson, Andrew S., and Lyle J. Goldstein. "China's Future Nuclear Submarine Force: Insights from Chinese Writings." In *China's Future Nuclear Submarine Force*, edited by Andrew S. Erickson, Lyle J. Goldstein, William S. Murray and Andrew R. Wilson, 182-211. Annapolis, MD: Naval Institute Press, 2007.

Erikson, Andrew S., and Lyle J. Goldstein. "China's Future Nuclear Submarine Force: Insights from Chinese Writings." *Naval War College Review* 60, no. 1 (Winter 2007): 55-86.

"Faculty - James Kraska, JACG, CDR, USN." U.S. Naval War College. http://www.usnwc.edu /Academics/Faculty/James-Kraska,-CDR.aspx (accessed March 28, 2013).

Fisher Jr., Richard. "Developing US-Chinese Nuclear Naval Competition in Asia." International Assessment and Strategy Center. http://www.strategycenter.net/research/pubID.60/ pub_detail.asp (accessed November 27, 2012).

Fisher Jr., Richard D. "The Impact of Foreign Technology on China's Submarine Force and Operations." In *China's Future Nuclear Submarine Force*, edited by Andrew S. Erickson, Lyle J. Goldstein, William S. Murray and Andrew R. Wilson, 135-61. Annapolis, MD: Naval Institute Press, 2007.

Friedburg, Aaron L. "The Future of U.S.-China Relations: Is Conflict Inevitable?" *International Security* 30, no. 2 (Fall 2005): 7-45.

Gaddis, John Lewis. *The Landscape of History: How Historians Map the Past*. New York, NY: Oxford University Press, Inc., 2002.

Gertz, Bill. "China Sub Stalked U.S. Fleet." *The Washington Times*. November 13, 2006. http://www.washington times.com/news/2006/nov/13/20061113-121539-3317r/ (accessed November 7, 2011).

Godwin, Paul H.B. "China's Emerging Military Doctrine: A Role for Nuclear Submarines?" In *China's Future Nuclear Submarine Force*, edited by Andrew S. Erickson, Lyle J. Goldstein, William S. Murray and Andrew R. Wilson. Annapolis, MD: Naval Institute Press, 2007.

Direction Regarding the Continuing Resolution and Sequestration. Washington, D.C.: Department of the Navy, January 25, 2013.

Heckler, Garth, Ed Francis, and James Mulvenon. "C3 in the Chinese Submarine Fleet." In *China's Future Nuclear Submarine Force*, edited by Andrew S. Erickson, Lyle J. Goldstein, William S. Murray and Andrew R. Wilson, 212-28. Annapolis, MD: Naval Institute Press, 2007.

Housman, Damian. "Lessons of Naval Warfare." *National Review* July 23, 1982: 894-96.

Huang, Alexander. "The Chinese Navy's Offshore Active Defense Strategy: Conceptualization and Implications." *Naval War College Review* 47, no. 3: 16-18.

International Institute for Strategic Studies. "The Military Balance 2012." *The Military Balance*. 112, no. 1.

Jane's, IHS. "Enter the Dragon: Inside China's New Model Navy." *Jane's Navy International*. April 20, 2011. https://janes.ihs.com.lumen.cgsccarl.com/CustomPages/Janes/Display Page.aspx?DocType=News&ItemId=+++1208610&Pubabbrev=JNI (accessed November 27, 2011).

Kraska, James. "How the United States Lost the Naval War of 2015." *Orbis* Winter 2010: 35-45.

———. *Maritime Power and the Law of the Sea: Expeditionary Operations in World Politics*. Oxford; New York, N.Y.: Oxford University Press, 2011.

Krepinevich, Andrew F. *Why Airsea Battle?* Washington, D.C.: Center for Strategic and Budgetary Assessments, 2010.

Krepinevich, Andrew, Barry Watts, and Robert Work. *Meeting the Anti-Access and Area-Denial Challenge*. Washington, D.C.: Center for Strategic and Budgetary Assessments, 2003.

Lai, David. "The United States and China in Power Transition." Strategic Studies Institute, U.S. Army War College. http://purl.fdlp.gov/GPO/gpo17692 (accessed December 7, 2012).

Lewis, John Wilson, and Xue Litai. *China's Strategic Seapower: The Politics of Force Modernization in the Nuclear Age*. Stanford, CA: Stanford University Press, 1994.

Loewenthal, Robert G. "Cold War Insights into China's New Ballistic-Missile Submarine Fleet." In *China's Future Nuclear Submarine Force*, edited by Andrew S. Erickson, Lyle J. Goldstein, William S. Murray and Andrew R. Wilson, 286-303. Annapolis, MD: Naval Institute Press, 2007.

Mahan, A. T. *The Influence of Sea Power Upon History 1660-1783*. New York: Dover Publications, 1987.

Masahiro, Miyoshi. "The Submerged Passage of a Submarine through the Territorial Sea - the Incident of a Chinese Atomic-Powered Submarine." *Singapore Yearbook of International Law* 10 YSBIL: 243-50.

McConnaughy, Christopher. "China's Nuclear Undersea Deterrent." In *China's Future Nuclear Submarine Force*, edited by Andrew S. Erickson, Lyle J. Goldstein, William S. Murray and Andrew R. Wilson. Annapolis, MD: Naval Institute Press, 2007.

McVadon, Eric A. "China's Maturing Navy." In *China's Nuclear Submarine Force*, edited by Andrew S. Erickson, Lyle J. Goldstein, William S. Murray and Andrew R. Wilson, 1-21. Annapolis, MD: Naval Institute Press, 2007.

Mearsheimer, John J. "China's Unpeaceful Rise." *Current History* April 2006: 160-62.

"MK-48 Heavyweight Torpedo." U.S. Navy Fact File. http://www.navy.mil/navydata/fact_ display.asp?cid=2100&tid=950&ct=2 (accessed January 24, 2013).

Murray, William S. "An Overview of the Plan Submarine Force." In *China's Future Nuclear Submarine Force*, edited by Andrew S. Erickson, Lyle J. Goldstein, William S. Murray and Andrew R. Wilson. Annapolis, MD: Naval Institute Press, 2007.

Naval Sea Systems Command Public Affairs. "Navy Provides Updated Cost Estimate for USS Miami Repair." America's Navy. http://www.navy.mil/submit/display.asp?story_id =69153 (accessed February 22, 2013).

O'Hanlon, Michael. "Why China Cannot Conquer Taiwan." *International Security* 25, no. 2 (Fall 2000): 51-86.

O'Rourke, Ronald. "Luncheon Address at JHU/APL." *The Submarine Review* Spring 2012: 9-20.

———. *Navy DDG-51 and DDG-1000 Destroyer Programs: Background and Issues for Congress.* Washington, D. C.: Congressional Research Service, Report for Congress RL32109, February 14, 2013.

———. *Navy Ford (CVN-78) Class Aircraft Carrier Program: Background and Issues for Congress.* Washington, D.C. : Congressional Research Service, Report for Congress RS20643, December 10, 2012.

———. *Navy SSBN(X) Ballistic Missile Submarine Program: Background and Issues for Congress*: Congressional Research Service, Report for Congress, RL41129, March 19, 2010.

———. *Navy Trident Submarine Conversion (SSGN) Program: Background and Issues for Congress*: Congressional Research Service, Report for Congress, RS20017, May 22, 2008.

———. *Navy Virginia (SSN-774) Class Attack Submarine Procurement: Background and Issues for Congress.* Washington, D.C.: Congressional Research Service, Report for Congress, RL32418, April 2, 2012.

Obama, Barack. *National Security Strategy.* Washington, D.C.: Government Printing Office, 2010.

Office of Naval Intelligence. "The People's Liberation Army Navy: A Modern Navy with Chinese Characteristics." http://www.oni.navy.mil/Intelligence_Community/docs/china_ army_ navy.pdf (accessed October 10, 2012).

———. *Worldwide Submarine Challenges.* Washington D.C.: Government Printing Office, February 2007.

Parsons, Ted. "Images of Mystery Chinese Sub Prompt More Questions Than Answers." *Jane's Defense Weekly 2011.* May 26, 2011. https://janes.ihs.com.lumen.cgsccarl.com/Custom Pages/Janes/DisplayPage.aspx?DocType=News&ItemId=+++1187032&Pubabbrev=JD W (accessed January 24, 2013).

Patton, James. "Cold War SSN Operations: Lessons for Understanding Chinese Naval Development." In *China's Future Nuclear Submarine Force*, edited by Andrew S. Erickson, Lyle J. Goldstein, William S. Murray and Andrew R. Wilson, 270-85. Annapolis, MD: Naval Institute Press, 2007.

"PLA 'Sinks' US Carrier in DF-21D Missile Test in Gobi." *Want China Times.* January 23, 2013. http://www. wantchinatimes.com/news-subclass-cnt.aspx?cid=1101&MainCatID=11& id=2013 0123000112 (accessed January 24, 2013).

Qiao, Liang, Al Santoli, and Xiangsui Wang. *Unrestricted Warfare : China's Master Plan to Destroy America*. Panama City, Panama: Pan American Pub., 2000.

"Report to Congress Pursuant to Public Law 106-113." http://www.dod.mil/pubs/twstrait_ 12182000.pdf (accessed January 30, 2013).

Richardson, Vice Admiral John M. "Primus in Pace." Commander Submarine Forces. http:// comsubfor-usn.blogspot.com/2012/07/primus-in-pace.html (accessed November 1, 2012).

"Russia to Deliver SS-N-27 to China." *China Defence Today*. April 29, 2005. http://www.sino defence.com/news /2005/news29-04-05.asp (accessed November 1, 2012).

"Saudis Board a Chinese Ship in Search for Chemical Arms." *The New York Times*. August 28, 1993. http://www. nytimes.com/1993/08/28/world/saudis-board-a-chinese-ship-in-search-for-chemical-arms.html (accessed November 8, 2012).

Saunders, Stephen. *Jane's Fighting Ships 2011-2012*. Coulsdon, UK: IHS Global Limited, 2011.

Scott, Richard. "Conventional Wisdom." *Jane's Defense Weekly 2011*. April 7, 2011. https://janes.ihs.com.lumen.cgsccarl.com/CustomPages/Janes/DisplayPage.aspx?DocTyp e=News&ItemId=+++1186616&Pubabbrev=JDW (accessed January 23, 2013).

Secretary of Defense Les Aspin. *Report on the Bottom-up Review*. Washington D.C.: Department of Defense, October 1993.

"Status of World Nuclear Forces." Federation of American Scientists (FAS). http://www.fas.org /programs/ssp/nukes/nuclearweapons/nukestatus.html (accessed August 28, 2012).

Taiwan Relations Act of 1979. Public Law 96-8. 96th Cong., April 10, 1979.

"Test 71MKE Torpedo." Military Periscope. https://www.militaryperiscope.com/weapons /minetorp/torpedo/w0006155.html (accessed December 4, 2012).

"Type 091 Han Class." GlobalSecurity.org. http://www.globalsecurity.org/military/world /china/type-91.htm (accessed December 4, 2012).

U.S. Department of Defense. *Annual Report to Congress: Military and Security Developments Involving the People's Republic of China 2012*. Washington, D.C.: Government Printing Office, 2012.

———. "Background Briefing on Air-Sea Battle by Defense Officials from the Pentagon." http://www.defense.gov/transcripts/transcript.aspx?transcriptid=4923 (accessed October 20, 2012).

———. *The National Military Strategy of the United States of America 2011: Redefining America's Military Leadership* Washington, D.C. : Governement Printing Office, 2011.

———. *Quadrennial Defense Review Report*. Washington, D.C.: Government Printing Office, 2010.

———. *Sustaining U.S. Global Leadereship: Priorities for 21st Century Defense*. Washington, D.C.: Government Printing Office, 2012.

U.S. Navy. *A Cooperative Strategy for 21st Century Warfare*. Washington D.C.: Government Printing Office, October 2007.

———. *Naval Operations Concept 2010: Implementing the Maritime Strategy*. Washington D.C.: Government Printing Office, 2010.

U.S.Fleet Forces Command Public Affairs. "USS Montpelier and USS San Jacinto Pierside." America's Navy. http://www.navy.mil/submit/display.asp?story_id=70139 (accessed February 22, 2013).

United Nations Conference on the law of the Sea, 3d. *United Nations Convention on the Law of the Sea*. A/CONF. 62/122. n.p.: 1982.

"United States Submarine Force Organization." Commander, Submarine Force Atlantic. http://www.sublant.navy.mil/ (accessed February 21, 2013).

Van Tol, Jan, Mark Gunzinger, Andrew Krepinevich, and Jim Thomas. *Airsea Battle: A Point-of-Departure Operational Concept*: Center for Strategic and Budgetary Assessments, 2012.

Vego, Milan. "The Right Submarine for Lurking in the Littorals." *U.S. Naval Institute Proceedings* 136, no. 6: 16-21.

Whitlock, Craig. "Budget Cutting Spurs Hagel to Order Pentagon Review of Year-Old Strategy." *Washington Post*, March 19,2013, 11.

Wolf, Jim. "Update 2 - China Submarines Soon to Carry Nuclear Weapons, US Draft Report Says." *Reuters*. November 8, 2012. http://www.reuters.com/article/2012/11/08/china-usa-military-idUS L1E8M80YW20121108 (accessed November 8, 2012).

Wood, Piers M., and Charles D. Ferguson. "How China Might Invade Taiwan." *Naval War College Review* 54, no. 4 (Autumn 2001): 55-68.

Yoshida, Reiji. "Beijing Says Tech Glitch Led to Sub Intrusion." *The Japan Times Online*. November 17, 2004. http://www.japantimes.co.jp/text/nn20041117a1.html (accessed September 23, 2012).

Yoshihara, Toshi. "U.S. Ballistic Missile Defense & China's Undersea Deterrent." In *China's Future Nuclear Submarine Force*, edited by Andrew S. Erickson, Lyle J. Goldstein, William S. Murray and Andrew R. Wilson, 330-58. Annapolis, MD: Naval Institute Press, 2007.

"Yu-6 Heavyweight Torpedo." Military Periscope. https://www.militaryperiscope.com.lumen.cgsccarl.com/weapons/minetorp/torpedo/w0007747.html (accessed November 29, 2012).